Life's Garden
of
Weekly Wisdom

Life's Garden
of
Weekly Wisdom

Sandra Lindsey Smith

Park Point Press
Golden, Colorado

Park Point Press
573 Park Point Drive
Golden, Colorado 80401-7402

Cover design, book layout & typesetting by
Maria Robinson, Designs On You, LLC.
Littleton, Colorado 80121
Set in 11 point Chaparral Pro

Printed in USA
Published November 2014

ISBN 978-0-917849-35-0

Contents

Sharing A Well-Kept Secret ix

Week 1   Life Follows You 1

Week 2   A Multitude of Monarchs 7

Week 3   Explore Your Possibilities 11

Week 4   Ants and Plants 15

Week 5   A Lacy Valentine 19

Week 6   Are You Sure I Ordered This? 25

Week 7   Building Trust 29

Week 8   A Little Bit Goes a Long Way 33

Week 9   At Home in the Garden of Eden 37

Week 10   Just Press Play 41

Week 11   April Showers 45

Week 12   Build It and They Will Come 49

Week 13   Be Fearless about Fear 53

Week 14   Giving Is Receiving 57

Week 15   Contemplation 61

Week 16   Direct Contact with the Infinite 65

Week 17   Dare to Be Exceptional 73

Week 18   Fields of Feelings 79

Week 19   Hazy Days of Summer 85

Week 20   Drink Deeply 89

Week 21   Healing Hands 95

Week 22   How Do You Spell Jabberwocky? 99

Week 23   Communion with God 105

Week 24   Candle in the Wind 111

Week 25   If the Blind Lead the Blind 115

Week 26   I Am a Blessing 123

Week 27   In the Beginning There Was Love 127

Week 28   Life Is a Dance 133

Week 29   It Can Move Mountains 137

Week 30   Looking Through a New Lens 141

Week 31   Listen to the Whisperer 147

Week 32   Magnetic Thoughts 151

Week 33   Mirror Image 155

Week 34   Mad about You 161

Week 35   A Starbucks Experience 165

Week 36   Move from Headlines to Heartlines 169

Week 37   Moving with the Current 177

Week 38   Love, Laugh, and Be Well 181

Week 39   My God Is an Awesome God 189

Week 40   Picture Frame Memories 193

Week 41   Ride the Tides of March 199

Week 42   Real Magic 203

Week 43   Release 207

Week 44   Shift Your Perspective 211

Week 45   Shoelaces and Ladybugs 217

Week 46   Simple Acceptance 223

Week 47   Something Spicy This Way Comes 229

Week 48   The Calm Within the Storm 233

Week 49   The Delicate Art of Mind Reading 239

Week 50   The Sounds of Silence 243

Week 51   There Shall Come Gentle Rains 247

Week 52   Wake Up the Kid in You 253

Works Cited 257

Sharing A
Well-Kept Secret

My life changed forever when I attended my first church service about fifteen years ago at Bonita Church of Religious Science in San Diego. I had been attending a Toastmasters' meeting at the church for three years before I picked up a brochure sitting right under my nose all those years. When I started reading about Religious Science I knew I had found my niche in spirituality.

From a very young age I felt there had to be more than one way to reach God. There were little children all over the world with parents who loved them and sent them to churches, synagogues, and various other sacred places to commune with God. I never understood why only one path had to be right. There were always too many mysteries I couldn't find answers for in the Bible. I never understood why I needed to ask someone else to fix my life. I was in my own driver's seat, so to speak, wasn't I?

Religious Science filled in those holes in my thinking. A spirituality that believes in all sacred paths; that stresses each individual's power to make wise decisions; that celebrates one universal creator; that supports the uniqueness of each individual; and that reminds us that our thoughts, wise or unwise, create our reality—what a breath of fresh air, knowing I can make a difference in my own life through positivity!

My purpose in writing this book is to speak to those people who feel they are spiritual but don't fit into a typical church philosophy. Everyone has a sense of spirituality; some just haven't met it yet. If you are looking for a new way to view life, I invite you to check out Centers for Spiritual Living at CSL.org.

I also encourage speakers, ministers, teachers, and others to share these ideas in your own way to inspire other people. To this end, I invite you to explore one lesson each week, by yourself or in a group. I hope you enjoy reading these thoughts on spirituality as much as I enjoyed writing them.

So many people have influenced me, from fellow Religious Science ministers, to modern New Thought writers. Even jokes and stories on the Internet have had their impact. I have tried to give credit where I could, so please forgive me if I have left out any names or sources.

I would like to thank my Science of Mind teachers, Dr. Heather Clark, Dr. Jane Claypool, Rev. Jane Westerkamp, and Rev. Judy Beiter. Thanks also to Dr. Cynthia Cavalcanti for encouraging my writing both for *Creative Thought* magazine and for this book. Thank you to my favorite high school English teacher, Wanda Russell, who fostered my love of writing at an early age. Thank you to Meg Chaffin and Cecelia Ward for being my first proofreaders; to my first editor, Denise Oconnor; and to my like-a-sister, Maggie Covarrubias—thanks for all the great books. Thanks also to Karen Drucker for her inspiring songs and books, www.karendrucker.com. And a very big thank-you to the blessing of having Sandy Chapman and Park Point Publishing in bringing my book into its actual publication. I am so blessed (Great affirmation). And last but not least, a big thank-you to my husband, Gary, who has been my silent support through all of this.

Week 1
Life Follows You

Feeling our true feelings and expressing them as we feel them makes us healthy individuals. Hanging on to our feelings and suppressing them can precipitate illness. Hanging on to our feelings and playing the victim can make us uncomfortable to be around. So, be genuine, share your true self at all times and do remember to feel the feelings, move through them at your own pace, and accentuate the positive.

"Life Follows You," explains Rhonda Byrnes in her book, *The Power.* Perhaps more aptly put, life follows where you lead. She says your attitude about all that happens around you has an effect on your experience. If you are genuinely happy when people you know succeed, you are likely to succeed as well. So if you want a loving relationship, don't be jealous of people who have a relationship; be happy for them. The same goes for someone who gets a raise or gives a great speech. Be genuinely happy for everyone's success and you are more likely to attract success as well.

"Life Follows You" also reminds me of the poem "My Shadow" by Robert Louis Stevenson.

> *I have a little shadow that goes in and out with me,*
> *And what can be the use of him is more than I can see.*
> *He is very, very like me from the heels up to the head;*
> *And I see him jump before me, when I jump into my bed.*

What a great analogy: If there is light around us, we cast a shadow. Early in the morning or late at night the shadow is gigantic. The closer to noon, the shorter it appears. In the darkness it seems to be completely gone. I like to think of the shadow as an analogy to our challenges in life. The more light or attention we shine on the problems or worries, the more prominent they are. The more we feed them with constant angst, the larger they become. When the light is more focused, when we allow ourselves to turn to our higher power, the problems tend to shrink. By the time we settle in for the evening, especially if we have turned inward to meditate and cleared our minds and bodies of tension, if we have released problems into the Law of Mind—knowing the solutions are there—mindless negative thoughts disappear and we can settle in for a relaxing sleep.

Look at the focus of your life for a moment. Is appearing perfect the most important thing in your life? Is it what you do for others? Will your friends and family remember years from now what you gave them for Christmas in 1993, or will they remember how you made them feel when you were around them?

Life follows you. Growing up in Norwalk, California, in what was considered the poorer side of town, two incidents remain vividly etched in my mind. I remember being at a speech team party and someone asking if anyone needed a ride home. "Yes," I said, "I could use a ride." When my teammate inquired as to where I lived, she said, "Sorry, my mother doesn't let me go to that part of town." Another time, my speech coach was giving me a ride home when one of the other team members said, "Boy, this is a nice home. I bet it's the best one in the whole neighborhood."

The warm feeling I got from that last compliment has remained with me through the years. Because of it I try to remember to give genuine compliments when the opportunity arises.

Life follows you. Dr. Wayne Dyer in his book *The Shift* has a chapter called, "We Are What We Came From." Isn't it amazing how New Thought writers find so many ways to express similar ideas? In the book he remarks,

> *Since I didn't come from my culture, my religion, or anything in this world, it isn't necessarily so that I must be the same as my surroundings or society. But since I did come from an invisible energy Source that some call God, or Tao, or Divine Mind, then I must be like what I came from. My conclusion about my origination is that I came from Spirit, and my true essence is that I am what I came from. I am a Divine piece of God. I am first and always a spiritual being inextricably connected to my Source of being. (7)*

This points out to us the importance of finding a spirituality that fits us, not merely a church to attend. The sooner we realize this and allow the world to call God by any name it chooses, the sooner we will have absolute peace on earth. The world is indeed our family and various religions express that idea, each in its own unique way.

Louise Hay has published a book, *The Times of Our Lives,* which contains true stories of synchronicity, meaning, and purpose. Wyatt Webb is the author of one of these stories, "A Sense of Connection" (216-219). He went through many struggles with drugs and alcohol, but he worked his way through life and a career in country western music to become the sought-after speaker and therapist he is today. He says one of the deepest connections he'd felt in years was when, in April 2002, he went to the site of the destroyed World Trade Center. He had been told that the New York subways were unsafe and people were unfriendly, but he found it to be just the opposite. He came to the city wearing a huge cowboy hat, and everywhere he went people smiled at him. When he visited Ground Zero he was surprised at how clean it was, nothing like the horrendous debris he had seen on TV. He thought to himself, "How capable and incredible of people to come in and restore some semblance of order to an area that had been so completely devastated!"

The church next to ground zero was spotless, and the fence surrounding it was covered with hundreds of thousands of expressions of sympathy and love and respect for the nearly three thousand people from different countries and walks of life who lost their lives on that day. Such a horrible disaster, and yet it brought so many people together to mourn the lives lost and to celebrate those lives that were spared.

Life follows you, and sometimes it catches up to you. Make good use of the present moment and radiate life. Ernest Holmes, the founder of Religious Science, says this in *The Science of Mind* textbook:

> *Think, see and feel activity. Radiate life. Feel that there is that within which is the center and circum-ference of the Universe. The Universe is the result of the Self-contemplation of God. Our lives are the result of our self-contemplations, and are peopled with the personifications of our thoughts and ideas. Accept this without question for it is true.*
>
> *Nothing is real to us unless we make it real. Nothing can touch us unless we let it touch us. Refuse to have the feelings hurt. Refuse to receive anyone's condem-nation. In the independence of your own mentality, believe and feel that you are wonderful. This is not conceit, it is the truth. What can be more wonderful than the manifestation of the Infinite Mind? (307)*

The beauty of Science of Mind—and at the same time, the difficulty—is that we are responsible for our own lives. Once we know that, we can no longer play the victim. Life follows our lead, and when we come to those places in the road where we are unsure of which direction to take, that is the perfect time to go within and connect with God.

Week 2
A Multitude of Monarchs

Asilomar is a coastal conference ground on the Monterey Peninsula in California, and I have had the pleasure of traveling there for church seminars for many years. Monterey is also a well-known mecca for monarch butterflies, one of the butterfly capitals of the world.

Monarchs spend their lives flying from the Rocky Mountains in Canada, down into Michoacán, Mexico, and back again. One way is a 2,500-mile stretch, and it takes five generations of butterflies to complete the journey. How can they possibly pass on the knowledge to do this? It sounds like a higher power had a plan. Wandering butterflies find milkweed plants, which are poisonous to all monarch prey, deposit their eggs on them, and reproduce. The larva takes a few days to grow into a caterpillar and spin its chrysalis, then after a few weeks, bursts forth from its casing, waits a few hours for its wings to dry and veins to harden, and off it flies. Somehow, it knows to keep flying north or south during the migration, and the cycle repeats itself to infinity.

This is very much like human beings as they learn more and more, continually evolving toward their enlightenment. The butterflies' flights are part of the Divine mystery of life. Surely, God had a hand in creating something so beautiful.

Thinking about butterflies reminds me of resurrection, new life, changing from one form to another, just as each of us has responded to our own individual spirituality. Each one of us is born again to each new day, into each new life experience.

As I was returning home from one of those Asilomar conferences, I had a delightful reminder that there are no accidents. The night before my flight home I couldn't get my ticket to print out, and I couldn't figure out why. I decided I would leave a little early for the airport to check in with the airline. The shuttle dropped me off at Alaska Airlines, but when inside I found no personnel at the counter. I noticed several people waiting who said they were told the agents wouldn't arrive until three o'clock. "But my plane leaves at 2:30," I said. "I'm going to Seattle." No flight was listed on the marquee. Another person sitting nearby said in halting English, "I go there, too." We compared tickets and, indeed, we were on the same flight. She was twenty-three and her name was Star. She was from China and was going to Portland to become an au pair for two small children.

I figured there was something wrong, so I called Alaska Airlines. They suggested I look at the ticket to see who was partnering with Alaska. It was Continental, and that was the problem; we were in the wrong terminal. Star and I began our trek on an airport bus to the correct terminal. I don't think Star really knew what was happening, but I helped her understand we were in the wrong place. We made it to the other terminal, checked in, had lunch, and boarded just in time. In retrospect I realized this was no accident. I was in the wrong place so I could help Star. Spirit allowed me to be an angel unawares.

I think a multitude of monarchs can easily be seen as a multitude of miracles. Aren't those butterflies flying across the nation with such purpose miraculous? Aren't the millions of good things that happen to us in a lifetime miraculous? I looked out the window on my flight and saw clouds and fields covered with snow and thought about the wonders of God and the ability of people to partner with the Mind of God to bring these ideas into reality: babies, puppies, beautiful sunsets, landscapes in nature that take your breath away.

Rev. Dr. David Walker had a habit of sending out just the right e-mail messages at just the right time. He once sent an e-mail about a zoo in Los Angeles that was trying to breed some white tigers. The mother was pregnant, but because she had a litter of five, she delivered prematurely and they were so small they died. The mother tiger was so depressed they were afraid she would die as well. Sometimes, when animals are in such a slump, there are other mothers that share their babies to nurse; but alas, there were no tigers with babies, only piglets. So, the zookeepers decided to experiment. They wrapped five piglets in pieces of tiger skin and put them in with the mother tiger. They weren't sure if she would nurse them or make a meal of them. The photo in the e-mail Dr. Walker sent answered the question: there was the mother tiger, lying down with all five nursing piglets (http://www. snopes.com/photos/animals/tigerpig.asp)

If you are ever down and lonely and there are no baby piglets around, get out and walk in the sunshine. Walk in nature, go into your own backyard or to a friend's yard and be replenished by nature. The world is a beautiful place and sometimes we just need to remind ourselves.

We are, each of us, perfect. Every one of us, just like those monarch butterflies–just as we are–is perfect, whole, and complete.

Week 3
Explore Your Possibilities

Living life fully means exercising our God-given right to be ourselves, to be who we are. We have the right to express authentically. We have the right to accept all possibilities, even the "impossible" ones.

Explore your possibilities. Your mission is to live your life to the fullest, nurture others and be nurtured, be mindful of the planet and all living creatures, and share yourself and your talent with others. And I know you want to accept that mission. A Michael Beckwith card from his *Life Lift-Off Cards* inspires me. The front reads, "Accept Your Mission Impossible." The back reads,

> *There is an impulse within us all—a creative urge— that is compelled to manifest. We can absolutely trust it and yield to it, and as we do so we will receive*

*feedback from the universe in the form of guidance
and inspiration about the purpose for which we
were born.*

I don't know about you, but when I truly know I want something, and I can embody that desire, it seems to manifest.

Karen Drucker in her book *Let Go of the Shore* speaks of manifesting one experience after another as she was guided along her path of musicianship. When she wanted a job playing music (a job that provided regular hours and benefits) and she spoke her words aloud, someone within earshot opened a door for her. When she wanted to perform on a cruise ship, she applied for a job but never heard a word and almost gave up hope. Then one night she was playing in a piano lounge when a man sat down beside her and started singing. Afterwards, they had a conversation and, guess what? You're right. He was a performer on a cruise ship. She says her whole life has been like that. She had a dream and she never stopped following it (33).

I likewise feel very blessed by all the jobs I have held. It seems that one great job after another has opened up to me. When I came into ministry, it was right around the time that Divine intervention was telling me to let go of teaching high school and move on.

Most of us at some point come to the conclusion that something in our life just isn't working. It might be a job, a relationship, a doctor we don't feel right with. It might be a house or a city we know we need to move on from. And you know what? Sometimes it's very scary to move on to something else, but when we do, a new path opens up to us. The right people and situations just seem to show up.

Was it a little scary for my husband, Gary, and I to move to Washington State when I first became pastor of a church? You bet it was. Gary said, "Kennewick, Washington, where the heck is that?" I left a profitable job in teaching to take a job that didn't pay as much but was filled with wonderful people and a fantastic opportunity to speak and teach and feel as if I was truly making a difference. After a gift from my mother the first year and my teacher retirement the next, Gary and I managed. The move was also a gift from and for Gary, who took a consulting job that enabled us to live anywhere.

When you decide to move on, it must be for the right reasons. You should never do so only because you hate your current situation—for then, chances are you will bring many of the same negative circumstances with you into the next job or town or relationship. You see, no matter where you go and what you do, it is your attitude about the situation that makes the difference. You get what you expect out of life. "Attitude is a little thing that makes a big difference" (Winston Churchill) are words of real wisdom. So if you move on, check your attitude, and know in your heart there is something better waiting for you. Follow your dream. If you don't, you will always wonder, what if? If something is meant to be and you truly embody your desire, press on and expect life to unfold before you in its right and perfect way. Ernest Holmes says in *Living the Science of Mind,*

> *In the Colorado Rockies there is a beautiful valley from which many fountains gush forth. Each fountain is different, more water comes from some than from others, but there is only one body of water at a deep, subterranean level which flows through each one of them . . .*
>
> *Each of us is a fountain of Life. There is a God-pressure back of each one of us, a Life-force seeking outlet through our thoughts and acts. There are many fountains, many individuals, but only one God-pressure back of all (23).*

People sometimes think of life's purpose as being *the* thing that will make them famous or rich. If that's the case and it happens, wonderful—remember to be thankful and to spread the goodness around. But maybe our life's purpose is as simple as being a kind and loving person to all we meet. At my father's funeral, a poem, "The House by the Side of the Road," by Sam Walter Foss was read, and one line aptly expressed his purpose in life: "To live in a house at the side of the road and be a friend to man."

Perhaps that creative urge in you is about loving children and grandchildren, baking cookies, or tending a beautiful garden. Maybe it's about having a grand time while spending little money.

Your purpose, big or small, is to be happy in what you do and bring happiness into the lives of others. If you are convinced your purpose is something bigger, start meditating about what that bigger thing might be. Meditation lowers your blood pressure, helps you feel more rested, and when you go into meditation saying, *Show me what I need to know about* _____, the answer seems to come. Maybe right away, maybe another day, but the right thought about what to do will appear.

When I think of the fictional characters Gomer Pyle or Forrest Gump, I see great examples of people who were unafraid of what life had to offer; they just believed in the Good of life. Our mission impossible can become possible when we embody the idea behind it, trust God, and trust the process.

Week 4
Ants and Plants

Every new situation we encounter in our lives is really a resurrection into a new experience. When we move or get a new job, when we end an old relationship and start new friendships, when we recover from a health challenge, all these are real life resurrections. A resurrection is merely a change that requires letting something go. This chapter title—ants and plants—refers to things in life that are always just there (whether we want them or not); things we purposefully plant—not only nature's plants with roots, but thoughts we plant into our consciousness. This ants and plants concept fits well with the idea of multiple resurrections.

Now let's explore a few facts about ants. The animal with the largest brain in proportion to its size is the ant. They are known to be the smartest species of insects with approximately 250,000 brain cells. Ants began farming about fifty million years before humans thought to grow their own crops—one ant variety even raises mushrooms to feed their queen. In addition they are known to secrete hormones from their legs that produce preservatives that keep the things they collect from mildewing.. There are three castes of ants: the queen, worker ants, and males. Males live long enough to mate with the queen and then die, while workers live for forty-five to sixty days. So what lessons can we learn from ants? Ants work together for a common cause; they know the meaning of unity and being one with the one, as in one with their own colony. Ants sense their unity with nature. They have been around much longer than the human species, and what they do, they do together. There are as many ants as there are human beings on this earth. They live only in their colonies as long as they have a living queen. When she dies, the colony soon dies as well. Cause and effect—the queen is the cause and the effect is the colony. The queen dies; the colony dies with her. So we learn that life always goes on, if not in one colony, then in another (Wikipedia On-line Encyclopedia).

A major difference between ants and human beings is that ants stay genetically the same for a long time. They do adapt to their environment, which is why there are so many varieties of ants, but once adapted, their life cycle goes on endlessly. They are the great survivors, and in that sense, we are similar.

Consider this: I have a friend who always gives the ants in her kitchen a chance to leave. As she goes to bed at night she will say, "I'm giving you fair warning: if you are still here in the morning, I'm using bug spray on you." In the morning, sometimes they are still there, but most often they are not.

Although we are never sorry to see ants leave our house, they can help us remember to watch our negative thoughts. "ANT" is also an acronym for "Another Negative Thought." Just like ants in our kitchen, negative thoughts are something we can live without.

Okay, enough about ants. Let's move on to plants. There is more life to be found in our gardens; snapdragons, roses, tulips, and daffodils are some of the pleasant, beautiful flowers we plant. Sometimes, however, we need to do a little weeding to rid the garden of its dandelions or other annoying, pesky weeds.

Beautiful plants are like the intentional, positive thoughts we place in our fertile, subjective mind, waiting for the Law to produce positive demonstrations in our lives. But there are those moments when we've said an affirmative prayer treatment and turned it all over to God (or so we thought), only to find weed thoughts springing up—those nagging doubts about how our prayer could ever possibly come true—and it's time for weeding.

Plants, like ants, are also great examples of resurrection. Each year in autumn, leaves fall from the trees. Marigolds and tomato plants wither and die, only to reseed themselves and grow again in the spring, just as trees are flowering and sprouting new leaves.

The changes we make, the letting go of old conditions in order to be born into our new set of circumstances is, in essence, a resurrection. There is an old story, *The Velveteen Rabbit* by Margery Williams, about a little boy who is given a stuffed rabbit for Christmas. He plays with the rabbit for a few hours and then sets it aside to play with new toys. The rabbit is ignored for a few months, so it gets to talking to some of the other toys and it learns that toys can become real if they are loved enough. Then one night the boy's nanny gives the rabbit to the boy when he needs comforting, and from that moment on they are inseparable. One day, the boy gets sick with scarlet fever, and is told that all his toys must be burned. While the yardman who is to do the task is called off to do other things, a fairy shows up and transforms the toy rabbit into a living rabbit, creating a resurrection of sorts.

With every new resurrection a silver lining is revealed, if we choose to see it. Each new situation we encounter is a resurrection into a new experience—a change that requires us to let something go. So plant those plants, those positive seed thoughts, and don't let the ants (any negative thoughts) find their way into the garden of your mind. If you do this, you'll find those silver linings provide you with a wonderful harvest.

Week 5
A Lacy Valentine

There is no difficulty that enough love will not conquer;
No disease that enough love will not heal;
No door that enough love will not open;
No gulf that enough love will not bridge;
No wall that enough love will not throw down;
No sin that enough love will not redeem . . .

It makes no difference how deeply seated may be
the trouble, how hopeless the outlook, how muddled
the tangle, how great the mistake—
a sufficient realization of love will dissolve it all . . .
if only you could love enough you would be
the happiest and most powerful being in the world.
(http://www.livinglifefully.com/thinkersfox.html)

This statement by Emmet Fox speaks so nicely of love, and, as you may or may not know, love is a synonym for God. Sometimes the best time to go inside and really listen to the voice of God is when life's challenges seem to be virtually impossible to overcome. The Mind of God is always available to partner with.

Valentine's Day is that time of year when we value the love we have for family and friends. A play, *Voices of the High School,* is a series of vignettes depicting scenarios that happen in a high school setting. In one scene, "Mary and Roger," Mary is up on the roof talking to the pigeons, lamenting Valentine's Days of the past and how she has always come up the loser. She hates Valentine's Day. She was always the child in grade school who received one Valentine while everyone else got thirty. She goes on and on, criticizing lace and crepe paper and explaining how Valentine's Day hurts children's egos. She has spent five minutes ranting when Roger suddenly appears with a huge overblown Valentine card and says, "I hope you don't think Valentine cards are silly." "Oh, no, Roger," she replies, "I have always loved Valentine's Day." He then says, "Will you go to the prom with me?" "To the prom?" she responds. "You're asking me to the prom! Just wait until I tell the pigeons" (Dee).

This story points out that everyone, deep down inside, wants to be remembered, to be included. We all have times when we feel a little left out, and those are the best times to reach out to someone else, to consider who else might be feeling alone. The US Greeting Card Association estimates that over one billion cards are sent out on this holiday, second only to Christmas. So even though the love we are celebrating on Valentine's Day should be a love we are sharing the whole year through, it is good to be reminded to include not only our close family and friends, but also those people we don't often see. You never know when your letter, phone call, or kind words may make a world of difference in someone else's life.

In your own life, if you are feeling a little achy, or a little lonely, Dr. Raymond Charles Barker in *The Power of Decision*, shares this:

> *You cannot emphasize enough in your mind the fact that God is life, health, perfect action, strength, and vitality. The repetition of statements like that one causes your subconscious mind to respond by corresponding. (113)*

It is our Divine birthright to have a happy, loving life. The truth of our being is that we are each perfect, whole, and complete. Our true nature is beautiful, happy, healthy, and prosperous. Things sometimes occur that cloud that perfection, but when we remember the truth, goodness prevails. Dr. Barker says,

> *A healthy mind is one that actually believes there is more good than evil in this world. A healthy mind believes that there are more fine people than mean people. A healthy mind expects right action to be taking place, and when it discovers this not to be so, it is undismayed. It proceeds to correct the situation without fear or intensive worry. It is never bogged down in serious negative thinking. It is certain of itself and of its ability to handle everyday problems. (113)*

We are often headed in one direction with our goals and choices in mind when life presents us with a detour: the car breaks down, there is a layoff at work, or our son or daughter is in trouble at school. Here we have the opportunity to put our beliefs into action. Has the fact that the situation happened going to change? Will getting upset and screaming change the situation? No.

"A healthy mind expects right action to be taking place, and when it discovers this not to be so, it is undismayed." A healthy mind is certain of its ability to handle everyday problems. As a result, we remember that when the car breaks down, AAA is just a cell phone call away. When you are laid off, that is your opportunity to find a better job, maybe closer to home. When a child gets into trouble, you have the opportunity to spend time with your child, analyzing how the situation can be healed and avoided in the future. Dr. Barker suggests, "Consciousness is what you are, and everything you experience is the result of your consciousness, and your consciousness is always hungry for ideas" (123).

If our lives are indeed a result of what we think into them, then we need to be thankful for what happens, and consciously be thankful for the goodness that occurs. You gain more of what you put your attention on, so let that attention be spent on positive thoughts.

Valentine's Day and all year long, as we contemplate love we must remember that before we can express love for others, we must be comfortable in our own skin. At our spiritual center, we light peace candles each week and say, "The first candle is for the peace within us; the next is for peace in our families, peace in our nation, and peace in the world." It is the same with love; it begins inside and spirals out.

The space between my first marriage and marriage to my second husband, Gary, was such a gift. I learned my value as a single person. I started doing some of the things I had always wanted to do and never tried, like taking swing-dancing lessons. I didn't meet the person of my dreams, but I had a great time. I discovered I loved my own company, and that I had the ability to recognize my connection with God. I learned the message I was meant to learn: I am loved, loveable, and loving. It was shortly after I relaxed into that knowledge that Gary and I began dating.

When you embody love—and this is true of all God qualities like beauty, truth, health, prosperity, kindness—when you speak it, when you send it out, you attract it back.

A professor was illustrating a point in his class one day. He said, "I can tell you all about life in a few words: mayonnaise and two bottles of beer." With this he pulled out a very large empty mayonnaise jar. He then pulled out a dozen golf balls. He put them into the jar and then asked the class, "Is the jar full?" to which they replied yes. So then he pulled out a bag of pebbles and poured them into the jar, gently shaking it as he poured. He then asked the class if the jar was full, to which they said yes. He then pulled out a bag of sand and poured it into the jar, again slightly shaking the jar. Again the question, "Is it full?" Again the response, yes. The professor then pulled out two cans of beer and poured them in. He then said, "Now it's full." He said the golf balls represent the really important things in our lives: family and friends. The pebbles represent the other things we need to do: jobs, clubs. The sand represents the ordinary things that may not really be necessary. It's also interesting to note that if the sand had gone in first, not everything would have fit. Remember, the jar seemed full with just the golf balls in it. When he was done talking a young woman in the class raised her hand and inquired what the beer represented. The professor smiled and said, "I'm glad you asked. The beer just shows you that no matter how full your life may seem, there's always room for a couple of beers with a friend."
(snopes.com>urbanlegends.glure gallery)

Remember the important things in your life: family, friends, and faith. Give them the love of your presence, the gift of your attention. Religious Science founder Ernest Holmes says this in *The Science of Mind* textbook, referring to John 13:34, 35:

Love is the eternal flame of the Universe, nay, the very fire itself. It is written that God is Love, and that we are His expressed likeness, the image of the eternal being. Love is self-givingness through creation, the impartation of the Divine through the human.

Love is an essence, an atmosphere, which defies analysis, as does Life itself. It is that which IS and cannot be explained: It is common to all people, to all animal life, and evident in the response of plants to those who love them. . . .

The essence of love, while elusive, pervades everything, fires the heart, stimulates the emotions, renews the soul and proclaims the Spirit. . . . A Universal sense alone bears witness to the Divine fact: God is Love and Love is God. (478)

We're back to that again, that God is a synonym for love, a love that is always there. It starts from within and spirals out. Let February remind us of that, and remind us that the month spirals out to encompass the year, then encompass all of life. Sometimes it takes a lacy valentine to remind us: love, laughter, and life, that's what it's all about.

Week 6
Are You Sure I Ordered This?

There is a little child in all of us that remembers the magic of having no limitations. Just as little children look at life with awe and wonder, we should remember to do the same.

The late Rev. Dr. David Walker, when asked how he was, would always say, "Life is Good." What a wonderfully simple phrase, for no matter what may be happening in our lives, in this moment, at this exact time, each of us is alive. If for nothing else, we may be thankful for that. Dr. David's book, *You Are Enough*, says that too many people pick on themselves. When you finally realize you are perfect, whole, and complete and there is nothing about yourself you need to fix, you can then think of yourself in a positive way and start enjoying life.

So what is your conversation about yourself and your daily life like? If you had a rough and sleepless night, do you tell people about it hundreds of times during the day? If you are not feeling well, is that the topic of conversation with everyone you meet? Are you constantly talking about all the rotten things your family members do? If so, what is wrong with this picture? The answer: you are prescribing what you are describing.

As a teacher for some twenty-five years, I learned early on that negative behavior in my students was sometimes a ploy to gain attention. So I started giving attention to the students who were doing well, who were behaving appropriately, and do you know what? Many of my students started achieving more and behaving better.

As you describe it, you prescribe it. Try this experiment: Think of people who can really push your button at times. Experiment to see if you can affirm some of their positive traits, and let them know out loud that you are pleased with the way they are dressed or the hard work they've put into something. What can you praise? Dig deep if you need to. If there is nothing good to say, then don't say anything. Silently bless them for being alive. See what it is like to let go of negative energy. Ernest Holmes, in *The Science of Mind* textbook, says,

> *It is impossible to divorce spiritual understanding from the proper use of mental law. The Spirit within man is God, and only to the degree that we listen to and seek to obey this Spirit shall we really succeed.* (275)

How do we speak to and listen to God? We speak through prayer and we listen through meditation.

Because it is done unto us as we believe, we must change our thinking and our beliefs to change our lives. In other words, we prescribe how our lives turn out by how we describe ourselves and our conditions, and we don't even need to be speaking out loud. How often do we easily forgive someone else for the same thing we ourselves are doing?

Our attitude makes a tremendous difference in every aspect of our lives. Many universities have conducted studies that link positive thinking to a person's improvement in health and mind/body connection. In fact, modern medicine is affirming exactly what Ernest Holmes and other New Thought teachers were talking about in the late 1800s and early 1900s, and was put into words by Winston Churchill: "Attitude is a little thing making a big difference."

Week 7
Building Trust

As we embrace our oneness, we are reminded we are one with God, one with each other and one with humanity. Remembering this, we are taking steps toward peace in this world. Building trust allows us to recognize that oneness.

Divine Intelligence, or God, is behind all there is in the Universe. Belief in God is not something that is automatically branded on each individual like a postage stamp. The quest for God is like looking at art; each person who looks at a painting will see something different. Each person will have a unique feeling with each piece of artwork. We are not carbon copy individuals. The same goes for spiritual belief. All individuals must find their own path, something they trust and find comfort in.

It is not a question of whether God wants what is best for me, or wants me to succeed and be happy. It is a question of what

I want for myself. If the truth of God is that everyone is perfect, whole and complete, then you can make the choice to accept that as so. Even if it seems as if everything in your life is pretty dismal, there are always a few areas that are going well. What are the blessings?

In 2002 I was diagnosed with colon cancer. I had been married to Gary a little over a year. I went online to find out more about the disease and discovered there are stages of cancer, and as it turned out, I was in stage one. I went to my pastor who suggested I try to find the blessing in having cancer. Wow. That was a hard one. I decided I was fortunate to have discovered it early, and that I was fortunate to have so many competent medical doctors available to help me. I read all kinds of information on the disease, including Louise Hay's, *You Can Heal Your Life*. She talked about how some cancers are caused by stopping yourself from doing what you enjoy. I put some thought into what I enjoy doing. What was I not doing that would bring me happiness?

Theatre is what came up. I hadn't acted in a play in over ten years. I looked in the paper and saw that a local theatre was having tryouts for *Love from a Stranger*. I went to the tryouts and found a character I really liked. She was Aunt Looloo, the comic relief in a murder mystery. I tried out on a Tuesday, and on Wednesday I received two phone calls, one from the theatre asking me to come back for callbacks, and one from Kaiser telling me my surgery was scheduled for Friday. I went to callbacks intending to tell them why I couldn't be in the play, and when I got there the director asked me to read the part again. She then immediately offered me the part. I told her about my upcoming surgery and she asked how long I thought I'd be unavailable. I said about a week and she said, "You are so right for this part that we will wait for you." So, I got the part, the surgery turned out fine, and the rest is history.

It took a lot of trust to get through my situation with cancer, and a great deal of affirmative prayer aided my healing. Affirmative prayer is about trust. When we do affirmative prayer treatment, we know the truth about any situation. I knew the truth of my situation was that I was perfect, whole, and complete, that the right and perfect medical team would always be there, providing the best medical care possible.

When we remember the truth, when we know that friends and family are holding us in prayer, we are, in essence, healing the situation. We do affirmative prayer treatment, release the prayer to God with deep thanks, and then trust in the outcome.

So, how do we build trust? Trust comes from surrender, particularly when the problem seems insurmountable. In doing affirmative prayer you might say something like, "I may not understand why things are happening the way they are, but I know what I want will come about in Divine right order. I trust the process." That trust comes from within. Raymond Holliwell, in *Working with the Law*, has an interesting thought:

> *If we are to obey the Spirit within us rather than the conditions about us, then the Law requires us to first think things into existence from the within before we shall see them on the without. . . . If you plant a turnip seed, Nature does not produce potatoes. If you plant a corn seed, Nature does not make a mistake and bring forth a giant oak tree. On the same reasoning, if you plant thoughts of worry, the law you obey will give you something to worry about. It will produce more circumstances to increase your worries. If you think of dis-ease and lack, you will receive exactly what you are expecting. Whatever law you obey will in turn serve you. The most important thing then is to know what to obey. (171-172)*

What you believe in, what you trust, is what you can expect to come about. You see an ad in the newspaper, or a friend tells you of a position. Do you go in for the interview certain that you will be offered the job, and then land it? Or, is your attitude "I never get these jobs; I don't know why I'm even going in for the interview"? Perhaps that attitude is projected in the interview. What you are sending out is what you are attracting back.

My mom has a great wall hanging that says, "Trusting in God is not believing that God can; it is in knowing that God will." The trick then is to remember to trust that the Divine urge is moving us forward. We are one—one in mind, spirit, and body.

Week 8
A Little Bit Goes a Long Way

Science of Mind teaches the value of living in the present moment. We must be present right here at this time, in this moment. It does little good to agonize about events that happened in the past or to dwell on past achievements. We can plan for the future, but we should never waste time worrying about what is to come. Life has a way of unfolding in perfect right order, even if we don't believe so at the time. What is important is what we are doing now. How can we serve, to whom can we lend a hand? That goodness, that positive attitude is what attracts even more good back to us.

"A Little Bit Goes a Long Way" is a chapter in a book called *Blink* by Malcolm Gladwell. It teaches that you can learn much with a brief glance into someone's life. The author cites the example of an insurance company asking an agent to find out which doctors are more likely to be sued for malpractice. There are two choices: one is to look at their history—where they went to school and what is listed in school records as accomplishments or errors; the other is to listen to brief excerpts of conversations they have with their patients. One would think the answer would probably be looking at the doctors' credentials, but the reverse is actually true. More malpractice suits are filed not because of a doctor's inadequate resume, but due to a deficiency of caring and honesty (39-47).

A little bit goes a long way. You've heard the expression, "You never get a second chance to make a first impression." This can be true, but there are exceptions. As a teacher I have had many occasions to make a first judgment about a student on the first day of school. One student in particular walked in with moussed-out hair, torn jeans, piercings all over his face—nose, eyebrow and lip—and Xs inked in, all over his hands. During the course of the first few weeks, he gave a talk about what he was committed to in life. The Xs were for not doing drugs, or drinking alcohol, or having sex while he was still in high school. His first informative speech was about how he loved to write poetry and put it to music. He explained that every song a person enjoyed was really poetry set to music. So here was a person who at first glance seemed hardened and not willing to learn, but who was really a gentle soul who loved receiving an education. Don Miguel Ruiz in his book *The Four Agreements* tells us not to make assumptions. The person who comes off to you as angry may be merely reacting to some other event in his or her life.

A little bit goes a long way. When I first considered this I was immediately thrown back to my childhood when guests would arrive unexpectedly at dinnertime. My mother always invited them to have dinner with us. On those occasions, we were given the F.H.B. code. F.H.B. stood for *Family Hold Back,* just to make sure there would be enough food for the guests.

My mother was a remarkable woman. She was born in India, a child of Methodist missionaries, and returned to America at three years of age when her father was sent home to recuperate from yellow fever. Back in the states, he caught the flu and died. It is ironic that he should survive yellow fever yet die from the flu. My mother's life was a poster-child example for a little bit going a long way, and she continually reminded us of this. At six years old she would ride the trolley car down to the chicken farm and bring home a live chicken for Sunday dinners, as chickens cost less that way. The family lived on vegetables from their own garden, rice, because it was inexpensive, and soup made from the carcass of the chicken they'd had for Sunday dinner.

Just as my mother had growing up, we also learned to make do. As an adult, that was a consciousness I had to let go of. I don't squander money, but I do realize now that God is my source, so I always have enough for what is important to me and my family, for our wants and needs, and my abundance spills over into a reservoir for future desires. Raymond Charles Barker says in *The Power of Decision,* "Prosperity is the ability to do what you want to do when you want at the instant you want to do it" (97). When Ernest Holmes speaks of supply in *The Science of Mind* textbook, he shares that

> *I always have an abundance of money and an abun-*
> *dance of whatever it takes to make me happy and*
> *opulent. There is continuous movement toward me*
> *of supply, money, of all that I need to express the*
> *fullest life, happiness and action.* (263)

You see, that attitude allows abundance to appear. It appears so as to express the fullest happiness and action. It isn't about getting money to hoard; abundance is meant to be circulated.

A little bit goes a long way. Isn't it amazing how something as simple as a smile can light up another person's life? Or how a genuine compliment is a great segue into offering a helpful suggestion? And sometimes, something as simple as going within to meditate about an issue brings about an easy solution. A little bit goes a long way.

Week 9
At Home in the Garden
of Eden

Let's look closely at the meaning of the Garden of Eden and a few standard Religious Science principles to discover how unity with each other is the out-picturing of our unity with God—because, after all, we are all one.

We are told in Genesis that Eden is where God created the first man and woman, Adam and Eve. What does Charles Fillmore's *Metaphysical Bible Dictionary* tell us about this? He says that Eden is

> *a pleasant, harmonious, productive state of consciousness in which are all possibilities of growth. When man is expressing in harmony with the Divine Mind, bringing forth the qualities of Being in Divine order, he dwells in Eden, or in a state of bliss in a harmonious body.*

> *The "garden" symbolizes the spiritual body in which man dwells when he brings forth his thoughts after the original Divine ideas. This garden is the substance of God (Eden) or state of perfect relation of ideas to Being. The Garden of Eden is the Divine consciousness.* (181)

"The Divine consciousness." I like that phrase. When man is expressing in harmony with the Divine Mind, he brings forth Divine ideas. That is the biggest reason people pray. What we put into Mind comes about.

Healing Spiritually, a book published by the Christian Science Publishing Company, contains story after story of healings through mental belief. One of these stories is about a successful businesswoman named Margery, who was married to an equally successful man. Both were alcoholics. They had recently moved, so she had given up her job. Margery was tired of being an alcoholic and had vowed to give up drinking. She prayed one morning that God would show her a way out, even if that meant suicide. She pulled her husband's handgun out of his nightstand and had her hand on the barrel when the phone rang. It was a friend inviting her to play a game of golf. At first Margery said no, but her friend insisted. She said even if she didn't play herself, she could at least watch. As they were playing, Margery opened up. Her friend then started explaining the nature of God and how she was made in God's image, perfect, whole and complete. She talked Margery into reading Mary Baker Eddy's *Science and Health.* Margery did, and was able to regain a certain peace that allowed her to give up alcohol. She was able to put into Mind the desire to live in a manner that was healthy for her (6-9).

Isn't it wonderful when a person finds a sense of the Divine that is meaningful? *Oneness* by Jeffery Moses is a tiny book about the common values that tie religions together. Each major faith has its own way of expressing similar concepts, such as the Golden Rule, or honoring your parents. Those values hold also for honoring all life and property.

Spirituality is practicing mindfulness. It is the *experience* of God rather than discussions and opinions about God. We don't want to force other people to think a certain way; we want to teach them to think and ask questions about their faith, rather than blindly accept something handed down to them. We endeavor to find our commonality through the practice of spirituality and unity with one another and with God. This sense of unity is a word that comes from God, and it comes from each of us as we recognize the thread of truth that unites all spiritual beliefs.

What does it mean to be united? The glossary in *The Science of Mind* textbook defines unity as

> *The Oneness of God and Man. The word unity signifies the union of parts, a result of many drawn together into one perfect harmonious whole . . . Oneness . . . One life, of which we are a part; One intelligence, which we use; One Substance, which is brought into manifold manifestation; One Principle, as Jesus taught: "That they may be one, even as Thou, Father, art in me and I in Thee, and they also in us"* (640).

I see that as being one with God, and one with each other, working with each other for a common goal or a common purpose. Coming together with God is also a way to achieve Divine inspiration.

So in understanding that the Garden of Eden symbolizes the body of Divine ideas—what comes about when we are in harmony with our true God essence—humanity can wake up to finding harmony with all people and nations. It is time we recognize that, truly know it. This is what peace on earth is all about. The Garden of Eden is our Divine consciousness. Knowing that, it is easy to be at home in the Garden of Eden.

Week 10
Just Press Play

Have you ever noticed that we just take ourselves too seriously at times? From time to time we are so focused on one small detail that we forget to see the bigger picture around us, or vice versa—we are aware of the world around us, but we fail to see the butterfly emerging from its cocoon. Little children notice everything, and each new thing they learn is a miracle. Over the years as we grow up, sometimes that fun-loving ability to play is stomped out of us. We hear the words, "Grow up," or "You're too old to be acting like that." Okay, which is it—am I too old, or not old enough? No matter how old we become, we must never let go of our sense of wonder.

By pushing the "play" button in your life, you are agreeing to be an active participant. Have you heard the expression, you are as young as you feel? Actually, to anyone who is thirty years or older, it sometimes seems like the older you get, the younger you seem. What keeps us young? Sitting around doing nothing? No. We stay young by keeping active and staying involved.

Many great spiritual leaders have shared that being in service to others is what life is all about:

The fragrance always remains on the hand that gives the rose.
– Gandhi

I am a little pencil in the hand of a writing God
who is sending a love letter to the world.
– Mother Teresa

I am only one, but I am one.
I cannot do everything, but I can do something.
And I will not let what I cannot do interfere with what I can do.
– Edward Everett Hale, Unity minister, son of Nathan Hale
(http://www.brainyquote.com/quotes/t.html)

We should never feel that what we have to offer is insignificant. That person who needs a listening ear, those cookies you bake for a child's classroom, that invitation extended to someone to share an afternoon with you, those are the little things that make a big difference.

What a good reminder to praise the abilities we have instead of lamenting what we can no longer do. I may not be able at this point in my life to run a marathon, but I can walk a few laps in the local mall three or four times a week. You may not have received straight As in school, but if you gave it your best try, you can be proud of whatever grade you received.

Be a participant in life. Push the play button and agree to see the best in any situation, and be amazed by what you see. This may mean remembering to respond instead of reacting to a volatile situation. You will not undo the damage done by a teenager's first car accident by yelling, but with your measured response, the teen can learn from the experience and avoid a worse mistake later.

How often do we tell that significant other person in our lives how amazing he or she is? Comedian Billy Crystal speaks of an argument he had with his father one night and the horrible last words he yelled as his dad was getting ready to leave for an evening of bowling. He regretted the outburst and went to find his dad to apologize, only to realize he was already gone. He thought, "Oh well, I'll apologize when he gets home." That was the night his father died of a heart attack (*Reader's Digest*, December 2005). Let the last words out of your mouth as you leave each morning be words of love and caring. See the best in people and situations and remember to be amazed at how wonderful they really are.

By pushing the play button you are both the student and the teacher. Who in your life inspired you? Was it a teacher, a parent, a famous sports figure, or humanitarian? In whose life do you make a difference? Anyone who has ever taught a class knows he is not only teaching the students, but the students are teaching the teacher as well. If students are young and a little squirrelly, they may be teaching us to have patience. No matter our age, we all learn from one another.

In whose life do you make a difference? What you do for another person may seem small and insignificant, but actually, you may have made a world of difference for that person.

As you push the play button, you are agreeing to be an active participant in life. You are agreeing to see the best in any situation and to be amazed by what you see. When pushing that play button you are both the student and the teacher. And, you are a difference maker.

Week 11
April Showers

Consider a couple of age-old expressions: "April showers bring May flowers," and "Into every life a little rain must fall."

It may not always seem so, but we can handle anything that crosses our paths. We are competent and capable, and God is always on our side. Situations may arise that we do not have control over—a flood, an earthquake—but we *can* control how we respond to those circumstances.

God never gives us more than we can handle. What happens when you lose a job, or when events transpire that aren't to your liking? A card in the Law of Attraction deck by Esther and Jerry Hicks entitled "Ask and It is Given" reads

> *I will do my best to make the best of it. A key to regaining your feeling of empowerment is to decide, right now, that no matter how good or bad you are feeling,*

you are going to do your best to make the best of it.
Do that again and again, and in a short period of time
you will find yourself in a very good-feeling place.

Ernest Holmes says, "Act as though I am and I will be" (*Science of Mind,* 307). Our attitude is what helps us discover the silver linings. A man who labored for years looking for diamonds in a cave not far from his home had lost his wife and family because he was so determined to find riches beyond his wildest dreams. One day he had worked very hard, became extremely tired, tripped, and found himself flat on his back, staring up at thousands of diamonds above his head. But at this point he was too old and worn out to do anything but lie there. He'd worked all his life without realizing the wealth that was his wife and family, only to die alone in a diamond mine. He never was thankful for what he had because he was so focused on acquiring "things." Had his attitude been different, had he invited his friends and family to help him in the mine, perhaps his wealth could have been realized and shared. He missed the silver lining (Cornell).

What happens when things don't go your way? You can give up and mope about, or you can choose to believe that Divine right action has taken place and something even better is waiting in the wings. Remember, God is always right where you are. Do an affirmative prayer and ask God to help you supply the right idea: "God, I could use a little inspiration here." Dr. Holmes states in his book *This Thing Called You* that

> *to realize God is ever-present, ever-available, is to*
> *know that all the wisdom, intelligence and power of*
> *the universe is right where you are. Your word is*
> *power when you know this. This is why everything*
> *in your life depends upon your belief, why it is done*
> *unto you as you believe. Change your belief and you*
> *can change your world.* (34)

So, affirm that everything is turning out exactly as it should. Know that Divine right action always takes place and is working toward your good. When someone asks me how things are going and I have had a particularly challenging day, I very often respond with, "Unbelievable." I am not going to plug myself in to a negative attitude. When I hear someone say, "Oh no, the flu is going around," I affirm in a loud voice, "And I am absolutely healthy."

Isn't it true, that each day is a gift? I love the saying, "Today is a gift, that's why they call it the present." The more we can stay in the moment and enjoy what is unfolding before us without dread of the future or regret about the past, the happier we are. God created us to be happy with life. If there are changes needed in your life to realize that goodness, then take the steps toward change. Start by affirming that life is perfect.

> *The only survivor of a shipwreck washed up on a small, uninhabited island. He prayed feverishly for God to rescue him, and every day he scanned the horizon for help, but none seemed forthcoming. Exhausted, he eventually managed to build a little hut out of driftwood to protect him from the elements and to store his few possessions. But then one day, after scavenging for food, he arrived home to find his little hut in flames, with the smoke rolling up to the sky. The worst had happened; everything was lost. He was stung with grief and anger.*

> *"God, how could you do this to me!" he cried.*

> *Early the next day, however, he was awakened by the sound of a ship that was approaching the island. It had come to rescue him.*

> *"How did you know I was here?" asked the weary man of his rescuers.*

"We saw your smoke signal," they replied.

Never forget, blessings do come in disguise!!
(Inspireme.net)

Into our lives sometimes a little rain does fall, but if we put our trust in God, if we know that with God all things are possible, then the clouds' silver linings come shining through. "Look for the silver lining," to me means, even when we perceive life to be less than perfect, there always seems to be a little good that comes about as a result of any challenge. It might take days, weeks, or even years, but eventually we realize everything happens in our lives for a reason. And besides, without the rain we could never recognize a rainbow.

Week 12
Build It and They Will Come

Who would have thought that going to a Toastmasters' meeting would eventually lead me to attending a Religious Science Church? When I mentioned this to a friend, he said, "You know the old saying, 'When the student is ready the teacher will come.'"

Build it and they will come is similar to that line from the movie *Field of Dreams,* where an Iowa corn farmer, hearing voices, interprets them as a command to build a baseball diamond in his fields. He does, and the old Chicago Black Sox show up.

But actually, that concept is what Science of Mind is all about, visualizing your dreams into manifestation. That's what Ernest Holmes meant in *The Science of Mind* textbook when he said, "New Thoughts create new conditions" (406). In other words, our thoughts create our realities.

Without this understanding it is easy to play the victim or blame someone else for our problems. But once we know we create our own experience in our partnership with God, we can speak to and listen to the voice of God, speak through our prayer treatment, and listen through our meditation. God is personal to each person; each person has his or her own special connection to God.

An interesting question to ask is, Do we find God, or does God find us? When we are ready, I think the voice of God speaks to us. Just as a wave is part of the ocean, we too are a part of God. A wave is not the whole ocean, but it couldn't be a wave without the ocean. A grain of sand cannot be the entire beach; it relies on the unity of millions and billions of other grains. Our spiritual unity encompasses all faiths. One faith is not God; all faiths are in, of, and through God. Some day, all people will know this—and that is the day we will have peace on earth.

> *A little boy was visiting his grandparents on their farm. He was given a slingshot and was out in the woods practicing with it, but he couldn't find a target. He was a little discouraged, but on the way home he saw Grandma's pet duck. Just out of impulse he shot the slingshot at it and the duck died. In a panic he hid the duck under the woodpile only to turn around and realize that his sister had seen the whole thing. At that moment, Sally said nothing.*

> *After lunch Grandma said, "Sally, come help me wash the dishes," but Sally said, "Grandma, Johnny said he wanted to help." Under her breath she said to him, "Remember the duck." So Johnny helped Grandma do the dishes.*

> *Later that day, Grandpa asked if the children wanted to go fishing, but Grandma said, "I'm sorry, but I need Sally to help make supper." Sally just smiled and said,*

"Well, that's all right because Johnny said he wanted to help." Under her breath she said again, "Remember the duck." So Sally went fishing and Johnny stayed to help.

After several days of doing both his chores and Sally's he finally could stand it no longer. He came to Grandma and confessed that he'd killed her duck. Grandma knelt down and gave him a big hug and said, "I was standing by the window and saw the whole thing, but because I love you I forgave you. I was just wondering how long you would let Sally make a slave out of you." (Inspiration.com)

Thought for the day, and every day hereafter: Whatever is in your past, whatever you have done or said, whatever keeps replaying in your mind—lying, unkind words, angry reactions—whatever you carry, know that God was there beside you, all around you, in you. Whatever it is, you can release the pain. The past is the past, and hanging on to it, replaying it over and over is the hell you create for yourself here on earth. Do not ignore the present because of past events. One day in a classroom at a local high school I saw a sign that read, "Learn from the past, live in the present, and plan for the future."

We do not have to go through anyone else to connect with God. God is all there is. The power is inside us, and is ours to use. Remember, as Dr. Holmes said, "There is a power on earth for good that is greater than you are and you can use it" (*Science of Mind*, 32).

Sometimes, in the hustle and bustle of our everyday lives, we get so caught up in getting everything done we neglect what is most important, like our family, for instance. Sometimes, we miss doing something we should have done and we agonize over it when we could be thinking, *In the grand scheme of things, ten years from now, will this matter?* Perhaps we can pare down what it is we do every day. Our presence on this earth is too magnificent to have happened by accident. We will find more joy in living if we make time for what is truly important, being with the people we love and turning within to listen to our inner voice.

Week 13
Be Fearless about Fear

How often have you found yourself in a situation where you need to tell someone something that's on your mind, but it's a little scary? Deep in your soul you know that unless you come out and tell them, the situation is never going to be resolved. The bottom line is that you've got to do what you've got to do. And when you do it, life becomes easier. One of Michael Beckwith's *Life Lift-Off Cards* says, "Be Fearless about Fear." The back reads,

> *As you become more fearless, fear itself loses its grip on you. You cultivate immunity against anxiety and doubt because you are no longer constricted by fear's energy. Creativity can then flow through you, offering skillful ideas, solutions and possibilities.*

Many fears, when faced by shedding light on the darkness they have caused, tend to disappear. This is especially true when it comes to secrets. There may be one thing that has happened to you that you believe is so horrible you would never share it, and yet when you do, you find people who are compassionate, and you are then so much freer. Admitting to an addiction can expose the darkness to the light. Realizing you are not alone in an addiction to alcohol, drugs, gambling, or sex can help you feel lighter.

You never know what life will place in your path. For me, going through a divorce was the opening of my spiritual path. I let go of the fear of leaving an old relationship and lovingly chose to be fearless about creating new chapters in my life. And guess what? Life brought me wonderful new adventures.

There is much in life that we could become fearful about: changing jobs, moving to a new town, paying bills, overcoming an illness—the list goes on. When we are fearful about something and keep obsessing about it, it becomes sort of like an egg that won't hatch. We sit upon it and sit upon it, but it never changes. The fear becomes a nagging worry, an ache that always persists, even at night. Why is this so? Have you ever heard the expression, "What we think about, comes about?" How can fear disappear if we keep feeding it?

If you fear looking for a new job, dwell on the steps you are going to take to obtain one—update your job application, find the perfect outfit for the interview, do an affirmation such as, "I know the perfect job awaits me. I let go and let God." Surrender it to God and it's done. You can let go of worrying.

If you are moving to a new town, think of all the wonderful new friends you will meet and the old friends that will visit you on their vacations in your comfortable new place. Do an affirmation: "I look forward with anticipation to meeting my new friends and creating exciting new adventures. I let go and let God." Again, you have surrendered it to God and you can become fearless about the situation and concentrate on other matters.

If a situation arises where you are tempted to worry, stop and think about all the other possibilities, like in the Twix commercial where two men at a wedding are discussing the bride: "Can you believe she's wearing white?" The father of the bride overhears this and says, "And why shouldn't my daughter be wearing white?" The young man who made the comment opens a Twix and takes a bite, giving himself a little time to think, then replies, "Well, sir, what I mean is that your daughter is so vibrant and alive, one would think she would choose a more colorful outfit." The father puts his arm around that young man and says, "Can I buy you a beer?" When the other man says, "I'd like one," the father replies, "I wasn't talking to you," and walks off with the first man under his arm.

That moment taken for a bite of the Twix is a reminder of the opportunity you always have to commune with God before you face a challenging situation. Marianne Williamson, in her book *A Return to Love,* reminds us that

> our deepest fear is not that we are inadequate. Our deepest fear is that we are powerful beyond measure. It is our light, not our darkness, that most frightens us. We ask ourselves, Who am I to be brilliant, gorgeous, talented, fabulous? Actually, who are you not to be? You are a child of God. Your playing small does not serve the world. There is nothing enlightened about shrinking so that other people won't feel insecure around you. We are all meant to shine, as children do. We were born to make manifest the glory of God that is within us. It's not just in some of us; it's in everyone. And as we let our own light shine, we unconsciously give other people permission to do the same. As we are liberated from our own fear, our presence automatically liberates others. (190-191)

You are an amazing person with incredible talents to share. There is a wealth of knowledge, kindness, compassion, and wisdom within you. You mean so much to so many people. The more aware of this you are, the more thankful you become, and the more you attract to be thankful for. Release fear and embrace God within you. When you let go and let God, you are fearless.

Week 14
Giving Is Receiving

I read a story in high school by O. Henry called "The Gift of the Magi." It is usually read around the Christmas holidays, as it's about two characters, Jim and Della, who are deeply in love, but have a very limited income as the Christmas season approaches. However, they both come up with a way to buy each other a wonderful present. Della has beautiful long hair that Jim feels adds to her beauty, and Jim has a prized pocket watch given to him by his father. Christmas morning arrives and Jim is quite surprised to see that his wife now has short hair. She opens her present from him to find two beautiful combs. Jim then opens his gift to find a very fine watch chain. The irony, of course, is that Della sold her hair to buy the watch chain, while Jim sold his watch to buy the combs. They laugh and hug each other, for she knows her hair will grow again, and he knows he will eventually buy his watch back, and they both know they gave out of love. In the giving was the receiving.

The gifts of Spirit come to us in many ways. A talented musician friend and I were speaking about his hospital music ministry. He told me how much he receives when he goes to the hospital to play music, and I know that feeling is reciprocated by all who hear him.

Some people in our congregation created framed, stained-glass circles, each of which depicts a different world religion, to grace our six windows. Those who see these sacred images receive so much beauty—and those who made them share their joy.

With the gift of prayer we become connected to the creative force behind all creation. We are all loving creations of that Power. When we say the words in the Lord's Prayer, "Our Father who art in Heaven," we are accepting that heaven is everywhere, in every action, in every moment. That Creative Intelligence awes us, as we are a part of it. There are those times when we have our paths planned out and something else happens; life takes us on an unexpected detour. Many of those times we have asked for Divine guidance, even offered affirmative prayer. As we pray, we need to remember we are trusting that the Universe will provide for us in the right and perfect way, and that may mean the results could indeed be something different than we had imagined.

We are opening an amazing gift when we recognize all the aspects of heaven here on earth surrounding us. When we recognize our poor choices and drop the agony about the past, there can be true healing. Sometimes, our resentments about what others have done to us can be so powerful that we are prevented from living our present moments in joy and happiness. If something you do brings harm to yourself, forgive yourself. If something you do brings harm to others, ask forgiveness of them.

Past events cannot be changed, but finding the lesson in an experience is the gift that very often allows you to do things differently the next time around, even when it is tempting to repeat old patterns. What exactly is temptation? Is it merely something that turns us away from productivity, something that causes us to stop and think about the best choice in any given situation? Might it be a gift that allows us to see the light at the end of the tunnel, to see the blessing in every situation?

Everything—love, peace, good health, joy, prosperity, the earth, life itself—is of God. When we pray to the Power that created us, we know the spiritual experience we are having in this body is not the end, for we will all transition into a new experience.

Week 15
Contemplation

Reflecting on how things are going in our lives, and being thankful for the blessing of life itself, is a worthwhile contemplation that can create real magic both for us and for the world. We are all spiritual beings having a marvelous human experience. Everything that has happened in our past, whether we perceive it to be good or bad, has brought us to who we are today.

Out of contemplation have come great works of art—brilliant symphonies, stunning paintings, masterpieces in architecture like the Eiffel Tower, the Leaning Tower of Pisa, the Taj Mahal, and the great literature of Shakespeare, the Bible, Walt Whitman, and Emerson. All the greatest manifestations of all time began with a single idea, a moment when someone stopped to ask, "What if I tried this?" and then acted upon it. Any beautiful garden or noble tree started with a seed. All life itself started with the seed of an idea.

Contemplation is introspection, meditation, birthing an idea and allowing it to grow. Each new step we take to improve something that already exists enlists contemplation. Airplanes were first powered by pedaling, as if they were bicycles, and we've come a long way since the Model T when someone needed to crank the engine to get it started. When Hyundai's first car came on the market, it was one of the automotive industry's cheapest jokes. As years progressed, however, through careful contemplation of its good qualities and flaws, changes took place. Within ten years, the Hyundai Elantra was ranked the number one small car by *Consumer Reports* magazine.

So, if you share an idea that is laughed at by other people, do you stop pursuing the idea? Or do you contemplate it more, look into new ways to allow your idea to expand and evolve into something magnificent? Wayne Dyer's *Manifest Your Destiny* speaks of keeping your ideas to yourself, and not sharing them with others. He says sharing them with others only gives them the opportunity to be "naysayers." If you really believe an idea is possible, he encourages you to run with it (62-63).

Isn't it a wonderful feeling when you receive an answer to your prayer? Do you ever feel it's easier to make the simpler requests come through before the major ones? Some of us may be further along than others, with more of our major affirmative prayers demonstrating in our lives. So much depends on what we are sure of, and the conviction we put behind our desires. It is amazing how much comes from allowing ourselves the gift of quiet contemplation—it is a very direct and powerful way to get clear on exactly what we want before we treat for it. Religious Science founder Ernest Holmes, in *The Science of Mind* textbook, succinctly says,

> *If one wishes to demonstrate prosperity, he must*
> *first have a consciousness of prosperity; if he wishes*
> *health, he must embody the idea of health. This is*
> *more than faith; it is the knowledge that we are*
> *dealing with the Law.* (143)

As I mentioned earlier, contemplation is a synonym for meditation, though there is a difference. Meditation is a time to quiet your mind, to think of nothing at all and to bask in silence. Contemplation, like meditation, is associated with Confucius, Buddhism, and Hindu mystics, and also with the New Thought/Ancient Wisdom philosophy of Religious Science. Meditation becomes contemplation when you focus not on silence but on that single-pointed one issue.

Contemplating a question such as, *"What will happen if I try* _____*?"* is one way to come up with answers or ideas. One of my high school students had parents who raised her to have high ideals and morals, but never allowed her to be involved in any after-school activities. How would you know if your children have learned the lessons you've taught if you don't let them fly freely to test their wings by themselves? After contemplating this, I spoke to the student's parents, shared my ideas, and, in her senior year she was finally allowed to participate on the speech team. She turned out to be a national champion that year in persuasive speaking. We can contemplate all we want, but unless we actually try something and put a thought into action, we will not get what we are asking for out of life.

Prayer is a form of contemplation that makes a request. In her book *Dare to Be Great,* Terry Cole-Whittaker reminds us that

> *Jesus instructed us to ask in his quotation from scripture: "Ask, and it shall be given you; seek and ye shall find; knock, and it shall be opened unto you: For everyone who asks receives, and he that seeks finds; and to him that knocks, it shall be opened."*
>
> *Asking is necessary, because we have free will, and even God won't intrude where He or His help is not wanted. Asking for what we desire and need is the key that unlocks and opens the door to the fulfillment of our desires.* (83)

So we birth an idea, we contemplate all of its possibilities with loving work, meditation, and prayer, and then we act upon it. This is the inward process of forming the positive thoughts that create the real magic in our lives, and in the world.

Contemplation works every time that we reflect on our lives and are thankful for the blessing of life itself. But contemplation alone is not enough; it is the catalyst for the idea to move forward with something. I am contemplating what to do about ____; I am contemplating what to do with ____; I am contemplating how to allow ____. Then, "Treat and move your feet," which means, say a prayer and then take some action to facilitate the prayer.

We are all spiritual beings having a marvelous human experience. Everything that has happened in our past, whether we perceive it to be good or bad, has brought us to who we are today. We are perfect, whole, and complete, just the way we are. A poem I wrote sums up for me the beauty that comes from contemplation and introspection:

> *Thoughts swirling,*
> *Out of the darkness comes "I Am," and there is*
> *brilliant light,*
> *I think, I imagine, I know...*
> *I create, I help build,*
> *I am kindness, truth, peace,*
> *I inspire, I attract,*
> *I make a difference—*
> *My expressions leave impressions.*
> *I am a microcosm in the macrocosm.*
> *I am a catalyst for positive change.*

Week 16
Direct Contact with
the Infinite

"Direct Contact with the Infinite," is the title of a chapter from Ernest Holmes's book, *Living the Science of Mind*. It reminds me of Cape Canaveral and space flight, or sci-fi movies, but it denotes the simple truth that we have direct contact with a Higher Power. We have a truly awesome reminder of the Divine Intelligence behind all creation when we contemplate the Universe that surrounds us, and the multiple Universes beyond that. From *Living the Science of Mind* we learn that

> *when we know there is but One Spirit in the entire*
> *Universe we shall know that there is but one Source*
> *for all forms. We shall know that every form is some*
> *manifestation of this Source.*

*When we have found that this Source is also centered
in us we shall know that we can come directly to It
and, discerning that Its 'Spiritual Nature' is Love,
Truth and Beauty, and particularly that It is respon-
sive, we shall make known our requests with thanks-
giving, with complete mental abandonment.* (198)

Very simply stated, what we think about comes about;
our thoughts create our reality. My direct contact, your direct
contact with the Infinite, is the tool we need to manifest every
aspect of our lives. Sometimes it's difficult in the hectic activity
of our lives to find time to sit in silence and connect. According
to Dr. Wayne Dyer,

*Connect with the Universe, give yourself permission
to get away so that you can camp in the outdoors;
swim in a river, lake or ocean; sit by an open fire; ride
on horseback; or ski down a mountain slope. Wherever you live, you're only a few hours (or even moments)
away from being connected to the entire Universe.*
(Inspiration Cards)

How do we connect? By listening to inspiring music, watching
children play, or watching an amazing sunset. We connect by
reading an inspirational book or hearing a talk or watching a
movie. Perhaps the best way is speaking to God through affirmative prayer and listening to that inner voice that comes in quiet
moments of inspiration, or in trying times when suddenly the
answer to a challenge occurs to us. We must learn to ask for
assistance with things that need to be healed—relationships,
financial hardships, health issues. Put the circumstances at hand
into an affirmative prayer or go into meditation and ask, "What
do I need to know about this situation?" Then sit in the silence,
or just put it into the Mind of God and let it go. So often I do this
and a few hours or a few days later, the answer becomes apparent.
Trust that the answer will come.

We have learned through life experience that there are things in this world that work for us, and things that can cause us harm. When we exploded the atomic bomb, Dr. Einstein and a number of other leading physicists realized there are powers of nature that can be utilized for energy in a positive way, or used to destroy all mankind. Consequently, all nations must learn to live together in peace and harmony, using the power for positive purpose. Ernest Holmes writes in *Living the Science of Mind,*

> *Do not hesitate to use affirmative prayer for any good purpose and for all purposes that are constructive. It might even reach around the world. Let us then do everything we can to increase our own faith and conviction, and be equally certain that we are using this faith and conviction in everything we are doing.*
>
> *If you want to start a chain reaction that will help those around you—realizing that it must begin at the center of your own being—suppose you take time daily to say these words to yourself, very simply and sincerely, and perhaps repeat the process a number of times each day:*
>
> *"I know that nothing but Good can go from me and nothing but Good can return. It is my inward desire that everything I touch, every person I think of, shall be blessed and helped. It is my affirmative prayer, which I completely accept, that even as I pass people in the street some silent influence of Good shall reach from me to them."* (243)

But what if you feel like you've been through the wringer yourself? What if you just can't seem to find anything to be happy about? You must dig deep. What are you grateful for? Are you grateful you are alive? Are you thankful that you have three meals a day, or that you have a home to live in, or that the world around you is filled with beautiful flowers and wonderful sunsets? When you truly feel grateful for something, you can't feel unhappy at the same time.

During those times when you still can't beat the blues, try some direct contact with the Infinite. Go within for some inspiration. Start affirming those meaningful friendships, exciting jobs, and vibrant health. Know you are prosperous beyond all measure and that you have more than enough money for your wants and needs.

Your daily spiritual practice is the best opportunity for direct contact with the Infinite. The best formal times to spend communing with Spirit are probably in the morning and at night. In the mornings I usually spend some time in meditation, read a chapter or two of a metaphysical book, journal about what's going on in my life, and do an affirmative prayer treatment. At night I add to my gratitude Journal. I write down at least three things I felt grateful for that day. I have to admit that my spiritual practice started out with only my gratitude journal. Whatever you do, try to remember to maintain contact with your Infinite friend. Two examples of less formal ways to stay in contact are when you pass an accident on the freeway or witness or experience a disruption at work. Sometimes all you can do is send positive energy and thoughts for the highest and best to take place.

As you become more regular in your spiritual practice you will find that calmness of Spirit is always present. Some people have wondered if direct contact with the Infinite is contagious, and I would have to say yes. Have you ever been around someone who is cheerful, peaceful, beaming with health? That attitude can certainly rub off on others.

Random Acts of Kindness by Dawn Markova tells of a man who walked into a coffee shop in a grumpy mood. He brusquely asked for a cup of coffee, opened his daily planner and grumbled about his day. He sat for about ten minutes, slammed his daily planner shut and walked to the register. As he started to get out his wallet to pay, the cashier said, "Oh no, sir, your bill has been taken care of. Our first customer of the day came in and paid for his coffee, and the next five cups that were ordered." The man looked puzzled, and then suddenly smiled and walked out.

You never can tell what a world of difference a simple act may make to someone else. The Dalai Lama in *The Dalai Lama: His Essential Wisdom,* explains,

> *It can rightly be asserted that loving-kindness and compassion are the two cornerstones on which the whole edifice of Buddhism stands . . . we should try to help others, and if we cannot help them at least we should do them no harm. This teaching grows from the soil of love and compassion.* (8)

Isn't it amazing when spiritual truths ring true, no matter what the faith? All faiths at the heart of their teachings want us to be kind to others, value life, experience joy, be truthful and trustworthy, and serve humanity. All spirituality is meant to make the world a better place. We all believe in the same Creative Power; we call God by different names, but that essence, that spiritual truth in its pure essence, is there for us to see. The Bible, the Koran, the Talmud, were all written by people who were Divinely inspired. So many sacred writings of the past and present have comparable inspirational values. There is no one book right for everyone, but unless we explore them all, we will never know what resonates with us.

Perhaps one of the best classes we can ever take in college is a course on world religions. It was in such a class that I learned that the Bible, the Koran, and the Talmud all tell the same basic Old Testament stories, with each religion having its own prophet. Only by understanding the beliefs of other faiths, and accepting them as right for the individuals who believe in them, can we experience peace on earth. Spirituality is an individualized thing. My faith is not my parents' religion. They were good people and I love them for giving me a spiritual background—a background that helped me understand what I do and do not believe in—but my belief is individualized for me. And for me, direct contact with the Infinite is the definition of spirituality.

Dr. Michael Beckwith's book *40-Day Mind Fast Soul Feast* tells of a woman on death row who had that direct contact with the Infinite. As she began to replace thoughts of her imminent execution with thoughts about God, things began to change for her. She was allowed to exercise in the yard once a day. Her sentence was reduced to life imprisonment. She began singing in the prison choir. Today she is free and spends her time singing and speaking about the presence of God in her life. But she would have been free had she never been released from jail because she was already inwardly free. Beckwith says,

> *Today many people give themselves life sentences*
> *served out in the prisons of their own minds.*
> *They are prisoners of fear, jealousy, limitation,*
> *or ignorance.* (Day 4)

Only by letting go of those things that no longer serve us can we be truly free. When a friend gets that better job, or your neighbor builds a beautiful extension on her house, be excited for her. Genuine excitement for others attracts things in your life to be excited about. Be thankful for the prosperity in your life and be open to even more. Take those classes you've always dreamed of taking; learn to play a musical instrument, or to speak a second language. Author Louise Hay in *Gratitude: A Way of Life* imparts,

> *I have noticed that the Universe loves gratitude.*
> *The more grateful you are, the more goodies you get.*
> *I don't mean only material things. I mean all the*
> *people, places and experiences that make life so*
> *wonderfully worth living. You know how great you*
> *feel when your life is filled with love, joy and health*
> *and creativity, and you get the green lights and*
> *parking spaces. This is how our lives are meant to be*

lived. The Universe is a generous, abundant giver, and it likes to be appreciated. (1)

She reminds us in her book to be thankful for everything, for even the low points offer opportunities to grow stronger or learn new things. So in our direct contact we remember to ask for guidance or new ideas when we need them, we sit in the silence to refresh our souls, we remember to be grateful for every aspect of our lives, and to share kindness and be of service to others.

Today is an excellent time to establish *your* direct and personal contact with the Infinite.

Week 17
Dare to Be Exceptional

When you are right in the middle of summer, especially when out on the river watching hydroplane races, or at the beach, or in Palm Springs, you know it's hot out there underneath the sizzling sun. I once drove past a church in my neighborhood where the message on the marquee read, "You think it's hot here?" I assumed they were making reference to the Christian church's version of the hereafter.

Religious Science is a little different in its belief about the hereafter. We don't believe there is an eternal heat-wave locality after death. We believe the only heaven and hell we experience are the ones we create for ourselves here on earth. It may be hot during the summer, but as a message I read on another marquee said, "Remember when you were complaining about how cold it was?"

Dare to be exceptional. Another good synonym for the word exceptional is *extraordinary,* which if you break it down, it becomes *extra-ordinary.* What does that mean? It could simply mean "kicking it up a notch," as the famous Italian television chef Emeril Lagasse says.

When I first came to Religious Science and heard the pastor talk about tithing, I began to squirm. I had the same reaction about money in every church I had ever attended. At an early age my mother taught me that a person was supposed to tithe 10 percent of her income—but I never bought into that. After all, I was barely making ends meet as it was. Well, our pastor did a program called "Adventures in Faith" that ended up with a call to pledge. She said to bump up your contribution a notch by giving an extra dollar or two and see if it made a difference. For me it did. It took three years to reach 10 percent, but when I did, I discovered that my end-of-year tax return amounted to just about what I had tithed during the year. When I wasn't thinking lack, I wasn't experiencing it. So you see, being exceptional, or extra-ordinary, helped me raise my prosperity consciousness, just by bumping it up a notch.

When we say the phrase "Dare to be exceptional," we could be talking about being exceptionally courageous, or wealthy, or healthy, or fit, or content. All it takes is a decision. Being courageous is sometimes difficult, especially when you are in a group of people who are doing something you feel is unjust. Do you stand by and not get involved, or do you speak up and try to remedy the injustice? I think of that great movie *Norma Rae,* in which Sally Field portrays the woman who fought to establish labor unions in the women's clothing industry; or Cesar Chavez and his fight for the laborers in the grape industry. Taking a stand is being exceptionally courageous.

Bob Proctor, author of *You Were Born Rich,* highlights eight men, all wealthy in 1923, sitting down together to have a discussion. These eight were the president of the largest independent steel company; the president of the largest gas company; the greatest whale speculator; the president of the New York Stock Exchange; a member of the president's cabinet; the greatest "bear" on Wall Street; the head of the world's greatest monopoly; and the president of International Settlement.

Proctor asks the question, Where were these men twenty-five years after that discussion? Twenty-five years later they were all broke or dead. Proctor theorizes this was because they loved money and used people, when they would have been better off if they had loved people and used money to do good in the world. That would have established them as exceptional businessmen (182-183).

Who doesn't want to be exceptionally healthy? Yet don't you know people who are always talking about this ailment or that? In the movie *Life as a House,* a man has a crumbling home on the beach in a beautiful neighborhood that he has been talking about fixing up for years. He is estranged from his son and his former wife and when he discovers he is dying from cancer, he finally goes about making the home repairs. In the process of fixing up his house he also rebuilds his relationship with his son. The man eventually dies, but he had worked with a focus that concentrated on leaving a lasting impression: a healthy attitude and work ethic for his son.

Dare to be exceptional. What does it take to be exceptionally fit? Rev. Pat Campbell was a speaker at an Asilomar conference a few years ago. She had released over one hundred pounds of weight over several years, and she told us the secret of her success: She gave up refined sugar, cut back on what she ate, and started exercising. Whenever she went out to dinner she immediately asked for a "to go" box and put half of her meal in the box to save for the next day. She looked fit, her talk was energized, and she wasn't exhausted afterwards.

What about contentment? What does it take to be exceptionally content? Maybe it's just taking the time to notice what is right in front of us. What have we forgotten to be thankful for? A man was at the seashore, walking along, examining the coast. He came upon a cave and inside found a bag filled with small, dried clay balls, hundreds of them. He took the bag with him and continued to walk along the beach. One by one he would throw a clay ball out into the surf. Then he noticed one of the balls in the bag had broken into two pieces. Inside was a beautiful gem. The man still had fifty or sixty balls left, so he sat down and cracked them open to reveal more beautiful gems inside each one. With a start he realized he had thrown hundreds of those balls into the ocean, and while what he had left amounted to several thousand dollars, he had probably thrown away ten times that much (inspirationpeak.com/cgibin/stories.cgi?record=153).

Are we sometimes like that man with the people we meet? Do we sometimes overlook them, or not recognize the exceptional value inside of them, perhaps because of the way they look or the clothes they wear? May each of us always look at the big picture and take the time to see things as they are, and not miss their value. In his book *The Hidden Power of the Bible*, Ernest Holmes relays some good information:

> *Could we see the mentality of a successful man, we should find the imprint of success written in bold letters across the doorway of his consciousness. The successful man is sure of himself, sure of what he is doing, certain of the outcome of his undertakings. As much gathers more, as like attracts like, so success breeds greater success and conviction is attained by certainty. The whole teaching of Jesus is to have faith and to believe. He places a greater value on faith and belief than anyone who has taught spiritual truth. We are to believe in ourselves because we have first penetrated the invisible cause back of the real self. We are to have absolute faith in our work because we have positive conviction of the inner power which enables us to do the work. (87)*

Dr. Holmes is saying that whatever we dare to be or do or endeavor with absolute conviction, we have the ability to do. There are few things simpler and more functional than the paper bag. Picasso painted on them; the artist Saul Steinberg used them to create elaborate masks. Four sides and a bottom, and no matter how useful it is today, it was invented only a little over one hundred years ago in 1883. Charles Stillwell, the inventor, was born in Ohio and participated in the Civil War. Shortly after his discharge he began tinkering with inventions until he developed the machine that makes the paper bags of today. Bags had been around before, but they were v-shaped and could not stand on their own. Stillwell had other inventions, but his claim to fame was the common paper bag we still use today (ohiohistorycentral.org/Charles_Stilwell).

The point is that we have so many ideas that could be so beneficial to humanity if acted on. Take inventory, jot down your ideas, and let one of them take wing. Remember, the only heaven and hell we experience are the ones we create for ourselves here on earth, so dare to be extra-ordinary. Dare to be exceptional.

Week 18
Fields of Feelings

Feelings can be fun and funny, or they can run deep and be quite painful. The important thing to remember is that the feelings we have, just like the thoughts we think, are things. They have the power to create, so how we feel or think about any circumstance in our lives—whether good or challenging— is how it is.

This chapter, Fields of Feelings, was inspired by Rhonda Byrnes' book, *The Power,* and refers to the energy surrounding each person, place, and thing on the planet. This energy can be either positive or negative, and it attracts to itself energy of like kind. So if I'm up and energetic and smiling with the joy of life, that is very likely what I am attracting back. When I think of the *Peanuts* cartoon strip, I'm reminded of the character Pigpen who always has a cloud of dust that travels with him. That cloud is representative of the doom-and-gloom situations following him around. Do you know a person like that? Someone who radiates a bad mood or likes to share the misery of his or her story, time after time after time?

The energy each of us radiates is what we continually attract back. Dennis Merritt Jones in his book *The Art of Being* tells the story of a man who left home and traveled far and wide until he reached a new village. At the entrance of the town sat a man who guarded the gate. The traveler asked him what the town is like, and the wise man responded, "What was the town like that you left?" "It was very unfriendly," he replied. "The people were mean and no one would ever help another person." The gatekeeper said, "I'm sure you will find this town exactly the same," and the traveler moved on.

A few days later a second man came by and asked the same question of the wise man. Again the gatekeeper responded, "What were the people like in your last village?" and the second traveler replied, "They were absolutely wonderful. I hated to leave but I want to experience more of the world. They were friendly and caring; they even gave me supplies for my journey." "Come inside," said the wise man. "You are sure to find many people of like mind here." (40)

What we send out, we attract back to us. The field of energy surrounding us is like a magnet. We give and we receive, and very often we discover that in the giving is the receiving.

Our thoughts create our reality. By recognizing the gift of each moment we can learn not to judge, but rather to be neutral about everything that happens. Rhonda Byrnes, a lover of flowers, said there is a farmer's market every summer in her town where each Thursday she buys flowers. But one of those Thursdays it rained so hard that the market was closed. She took it in stride and realized she would enjoy her flowers even more for having missed them one week. The next Monday, however, she was delightfully surprised to receive a bunch of flowers from her sister on the other side of the country, thanking her for something she had done. That field of positive energy surrounding Rhonda attracted another positive situation back to her (*The Power*).

Karen Drucker in her book *Let Go of the Shore* shares a time when she was returning from a workshop and her plane was delayed. She realized she might possibly miss her connecting flight and have to lay over for the night on the next leg of her trip. Instead of worrying, she sat down with a good book. Then out of the corner of her eye she saw a shaft of light. When she looked up, she saw a white baby grand piano sitting by itself at gate seven. She was drawn to it. She looked one way and then another, then sat down and started playing. Ten minutes later she saw a person in an airport uniform coming toward her and she thought she would be asked to stop. Instead, the young man was somewhat of a beginning composer and asked if he could play an original piece of music for her to see what she thought. They talked and played and about twenty more minutes went by when she heard her flight being called. Because she had been sending out positive energy, it was reflected back to her (71).

Rhonda Byrnes comments in *The Power* that

> whether you want to change your health, money, relationships, or anything else, the process is the same! Imagine what you want. Imagine and feel the love of having it. Imagine every scene and situation you can to be what you want, and feel you have it now. Try spending seven minutes each day imagining and feeling having what you want. Do it each day until you feel as though you already have your desire. Do it until you know your desire belongs to you, as you know your name belongs to you. With some things you will get to this state after just one or two days. Other things may take you longer. Then simply get on with your life, giving as much love and as

many good feelings as you can, because the more
love you give, the faster you will receive what you
desire. (e-book)

In paintings of ancient times or those by an inspired spiritual artist, you will sometimes see a circle of glowing light surrounding people. This is an electromagnetic field, called an aura, and some individuals can see them. I don't know if I can actually see auras, but I can tell you that in my twenty-five years of teaching high school, I have noticed the room being lighter or darker around different classes—usually darker around some of my more challenging ones.

We too, as individuals, have these fields of energy surrounding us. Feelings, positive or negative, have tremendous power and are an important element in doing effective affirmative prayer treatments. If you too often feel you get no results when you do affirmative prayer, then you will continue to get no results. But if you place your thoughts in Mind, knowing that an answer will show up, then what you ask for—or something better—will come about.

For my husband, Gary, this always works with his job searches. As he prepares to release one job, he starts putting into Mind the qualities, salary, or skill sets he would like to attract in his new employment. He opens his eyes to new skills he may pick up along the way. He trusts that the process of change will come about, and each and every job has been better than the last for him. Ernest Holmes shares this in his *Science of Mind* textbook:

> *We do not create the energy, we distribute it, and in*
> *the natural sciences we know that we can transform*
> *energy from one type to another. So the will may*
> *decide what form the energy is to take but it cannot*
> *nor does it need to create the energy.*

The energy of Mind like other natural energies
already exists. We merely use It and it is within our
power to cause it to take varying forms for us,
no particular one is permanent. The imagination
is creative, the will is directive. (193)

Gary and I were in Cody, Wyoming, an amazing place to visit. We drove a few hours from Cody to visit Little Big Horn and learn more about Custer's Last Stand. That trip gave us an excellent perspective on how the Indians tried to protect their land from the invasion of the US Army. It was a good example of how war brings out negative energy, with one angry event leading to another, and another.

Back in Cody we visited the Historical Museum where we learned about the town's namesake, William Cody, also known as Buffalo Bill, an excellent supplier of buffalo meat for the army. Here was a man who grew up supporting his widowed mother from around age twelve. He held just about every job imaginable for a boy his age, including Pony Express rider, noteworthy army scout, and historical performer.

We then traveled to Yellowstone Park and saw Old Faithful and other awe-inspiring geysers. All that beauty is a true testimony to a power greater than we are. We also had a wonderful experience during a one-hour rafting adventure that allowed us to face our fears and do it anyway. The entire trip awakened us to our fields of feelings. We found ourselves contemplating how we react to one another and to our natural environment.

What events have sparked deep feelings in you? The birth of a child or grandchild? Meeting your very first significant other (which in my case was the family dog)? Buying your own first car or house? Recognizing the areas in your life that needed to change?

The power of any feeling can move us forward: anger, joy, fear, love, desperation, hunger for peace in our lives. Positive or negative feelings can propel us into something even more positive. Sometimes, unhappy feelings are the very catalysts that spur us into action.

Life always unfolds exactly as it should. A student in my speech and drama program in San Diego graduated valedictorian of her class and headed off to U.C. Berkeley to study, of all things, accounting. In her second semester she took statistics and received her first-ever "D" grade. She repeated the class in the summer, only to bring it up to a "C." She was lamenting this situation, and I asked her why she ever considered accounting in the first place. She said her father told her it was a good career for providing a good income. "Brenda," I said, "you are such a people person. In accounting you will spend your time in a small room working with numbers when you should be working with people. Why don't you talk to your counselor about changing majors?" She did, and decided to pursue social sciences. She became a wonderful social worker and then proceeded to become a lawyer. If she hadn't discovered what she did not excel in, she probably would not have moved forward to discover where she would excel. The power of your feelings is much stronger when they are *your own feelings*.

Each person on this planet has unique talents and a field of feelings solely their own. As Ernest Holmes in *This Thing Called You* so aptly stated, "The spirit has set the stamp of individuality upon Itself and called it you" (86).

Week 19
Hazy Days of Summer

Hot topics my family did not want to talk about when I was growing up: my aunt Muriel coming for a visit; my dad's *short* accounts of anything; and my questions about why there was only one way to believe in God. Hot topics were always put on the back burner.

Sometimes in our lives, important issues are placed on the back burner where they simmer and bubble until they reach a point where they must be attended to or we will burn out. Have you ever experienced a summer that did not really feel like summer? Maybe an abundance of rain clouds caused the summer to appear hazy. Seasons keep showing up, year after year, no matter what. It can sometimes feel as if summer comes around again before we have cleared up some of our issues, and then life itself seems hazy and confusing. The dictionary defines hazy as

1. *Marked by the presence of haze; misty;*
   hazy sunshine.
2. *Unclear, confused, or uncertain.*

When life presents challenges we are often unclear, confused, and uncertain as to what we should do. Challenges don't seem to have age or gender barriers; they arrive on a regular basis to a wide variety of people. They can be about family, love relationships, finances, health, old age, not being old enough, weight and exercise, you name it; the challenges are there. They vary yet they all have one thing in common: They grow as we worry about them. As we nourish them with our constant angst, they flourish. We might even say, "Why does this always happen to me?" We need to see that we are like divining rods for negative energy. We can be like little nurseries, encouraging negative thoughts to bloom and grow.

At some point, it becomes time to take stock of your negative thoughts, time to say, "Enough! You are not welcome here anymore." Begin by affirming that life is good. Stop complaining to anyone and everyone who will listen. Negative energy attracts more negative energy; likewise, positive energy attracts positive energy. Try quieting yourself in turbulent times; turn inside and commune with God. The answer is always there when we remember to let God in. As Ernest Holmes explains, in *The Science of Mind* textbook,

> *Each individual maintains his identity in Law,*
> *through his personal use of It. And each is drawing*
> *from Life what he thinks into it! To learn to think*
> *is to learn to live . . . Man, by thinking, can bring*
> *into his experience whatsoever he desires—if he*
> *thinks correctly, and becomes a living embodiment*
> *of his thoughts* (30).

So, right thinking eliminates the haze. It focuses our eyes on the truth that life is good and so are we. We are enough; and there *is* enough for all of us.

Nat King Cole sang a song called, "Those Lazy Hazy Crazy Days of Summer." It begs to have summer last all year long. I don't know about you, but for me, in late July or August summer gets to be a bit much. And then, just as I bemoan summer, winter is upon us. A better way is to just go with the flow and appreciate the best every season has to offer, and the best life has to give.

I've discovered something I didn't know as a teenager: the older I get, the younger that older age seems. Forty suddenly becomes the new thirty, fifty the new forty. Age is a mindset. If we keep moving, eat right, and continue learning, we age to perfection.

In *Kitchen Table Wisdom,* a book by Rachel Naomi Remen, MD, the doctor tells of an eighty-five-year-old patient who came to her for some spots of cancer found on his lung. After a few days of consideration, he decided to have surgery. Dr. Remen concurred, and asked him how he came to this decision. He said he had a dream where his wife and a few of his best friends stood beside him smiling. Gradually people he had known from the past crowded the living room and extended out into the hallway. He said he realized his life had impacted other people. He had children and grandchildren, so he had the possibility of affecting many more. He also realized that whether he made it through the operation or not, friends were waiting for him, and family loved him. He wanted to live (165-166).

We all go through hazy days of summer, yet when we do, sunny, haze-free days always follow. Establishing the habits of meditation and affirmative prayer helps us share the challenges and be receptive to those Divine right ideas. Being thankful for all your blessings when life flows smoothly is a worthwhile habit. And especially when days seem a bit hazy, reach out and see how you might be of service. What we send out—the positive energy we generate with our kind words and actions—is what we will attract back.

I actually like the meaning that the word "hot" generates today. Hot can mean a good-looking man or woman, or an exciting topic. And sometimes, when it's really hot, the haze or the foggy thinking, is eliminated. Right thinking also eliminates haze. It focuses our eyes on the truth—that life is good and so are we. We are enough.

Week 20
Drink Deeply

Let me ask you a question: Do you get more done when you have too much to do, or do you get more done when you have plenty of time for a project? I know I work more efficiently when I have a lot of projects going on, but it's also true that sometimes, when I have much to do, I get so overwhelmed I have a hard time getting focused enough to start. I read an article on the Internet that I could relate to:

> *I think I have adult ADD—Attention deficit disorder. This morning I got up and I was going to take out the trash. When I got into the kitchen I saw that the dishwasher was done, so I started unloading the dishes. The phone rang so I answered it and the call was for my son, so I opened the drawer to find something to take a message with, and the drawer was*

messy. I thought I should take the time to clean it.
As I was sorting I found some pictures and thought
they should probably go into the photo album. This
continued for the rest of the day, one thing leading
to another. At the end of the day I hadn't taken the
trash out, I can't really pinpoint exactly what it was
I did that day, but I know I was tired. (Joke of the
day.wordpress.com/2006/07/23)

My loving husband pointed out to me that I need to make a
list of what I expect to accomplish each day, and I've discovered
when I do that I actually am more focused. Thanks, Gary.

In Religious Science we hear the words, "Being in the present
moment" quite a bit. It seems to me there is a little conflict
between being "in the moment," and obsessing with the past or
being lost in future plans. Many people have had the experience
of driving home when they suddenly realize, "Wow, I'm already
home and I don't exactly know how I got here." Maybe they meant
to stop by the grocery store, or pick up that suit at the cleaners,
but the car just drove itself home on automatic pilot.

Being in the moment means being present with anyone or
anything around you. The best gift you can give someone else is
to listen to him or her intently. Very often, if a loved one in your
family has a problem, what he or she wants to do is tell you about
it. Before you give an opinion or offer your thoughts, make sure
the person you are listening to really wants your advice. The best
solutions usually are those that come from within, and very often,
talking out loud helps a person figure out his dilemma on his own.

Drink Deeply. Do everything with your whole heart and
mind. Drinking deeply means taking everything in, examining it,
exploring it, and deciding for yourself if it is something you can
accept as being true for you. This could mean delving into religion
or education, relationships, current events in the news, or even
others' opinions about what's happening in your life.

Ralph Waldo Emerson was very much into self-reliance. His views on both religion and education were that they are unique for each individual. He felt too many people in society blindly follow what they were told instead of thinking for themselves. He would have agreed with the Science of Mind concepts of teaching *how* to think instead of *what* to think.

I think of my own connection to my spiritual side and how I came into Religious Science. I was forty-four, but intrinsically I had embraced it from childhood; I just didn't know what to call it at the time. We live in a diverse world so it makes sense that there are diverse pathways to God. Religious Science is one of those ways, and I feel blessed that I have found something I can embrace. To me this philosophy is a thinking person's religion.

In relationships, as in everything else, we attract back to us what we send out. The best way to have a good friend is to be a good friend. If you want friends, be proactive and put yourself into situations where you will meet people. Sign up for a dance class, take yoga, or a class on metaphysics. Say yes when you are invited to a friend's house for dinner. Ernest Holmes in his *Science of Mind* textbook shares,

> *Man, by thinking, can bring into his experience whatsoever he desires—if he thinks correctly, and becomes a living embodiment of his thoughts.* (30)

In other words, we need to do something with our inspiration. In Act II of the play *Our Town* by Thornton Wilder, Emily and George have a wonderful soda shop scene where they sit and talk with each other. Neither one wants to be the first to admit feelings for the other until they are sure that those feelings are reciprocal. The scene goes on for about five minutes before this realization comes about, and, when it does, they are washed with emotion, and then they laugh about it.

It is true that no one knows our feelings unless we actually share them. We must drink deeply—that is, examine our own feelings, but not drink so deeply that we drown. Eventually we must act upon our thoughts.

What about events going on in the world around us—the Washington Bridge falling down, the mine collapsing in Brazil? We do need to be aware of what is happening in the world, but do we need to be glued to the television, watching every replay of a tragedy, or reading day after day about the same horrific events? Whether we obsess with the news or not, the big events always seem to find and inform us.

Back in the early days of news, there was no bombardment of media hashing and rehashing each new battle as it was fought. Yes, we had newspapers, but not the constant replaying of negative events. Dr. Wayne Dyer in his book *Being in Balance* comments,

> *Let me tell you how I choose to respond to the bombardment of messages that focus on what's wrong in the world. First, I remind myself that for every act of evil there are a million acts of kindness. I choose to believe that people are essentially good and that by staying in this belief system, I help bring more of this consciousness to fruition. When enough of us take on this holy notion that whatever good we have is all from God, we'll learn to live collectively in this peaceful awareness.* (118)

Ernest Holmes used to read the paper each morning, then set it aside and say, "But that's not the truth." He stayed informed without buying into the race consciousness of doom and gloom. Wonderful things happen in this world, but they don't always get the front-page billing that other events do. Two hundred things may go right during our day, but that one negative comment, a comment we may even have misinterpreted, is too often what we obsess about.

A young man went to visit the Buddha planning to unnerve the wise man. He wanted to see if he could make the Buddha angry. For a week, every day, he would hurl insults at the Buddha whose response, of course, was to remain calm. Finally, after five days of no reaction, he screamed at the Buddha, "How can you keep your calm and control when daily I insult you?" The Buddha replied, "Because I never accepted the gift. If a person brings you a gift and you fail to open it, was the gift ever given?" (www.saibabaofindia.com/the_life_of_buddha_5.htm)

Life is made of energy, and everything within our bodies reacts to the energy around us. If we are in hustle and bustle mode all day, and we run into negative energy, we will be much calmer if we refuse to react, if we fail to buy into the negative energy. Meditation helps to charge our souls with inner peace so we can be like the Buddha who refuses to accept the gift of anger.

We have the God-given ability to choose the lives we want to live, so drink deeply of life. I was reminded in an e-mail of Audrey Hepburn's favorite poem, "Time Tested Beauty Tips" by the late humorist Sam Levenson.

> *For attractive lips, speak words of kindness.*
> *For lovely eyes, seek out the good in people.*
> *For a slim figure, share your food with the hungry.*
> *For beautiful hair, let a child run his or her fingers*
>   *through it once a day.*
> *For poise, walk with the knowledge that you never*
>   *walk alone.*
> *People, even more than things, have to be restored,*
>   *renewed, revived, reclaimed and redeemed;*
>   *never throw out anyone.*
> *Remember, if you ever need a helping hand,*
>   *you'll find one at the end of each of your arms.*
> *As you grow older, you will discover that you have*
>   *two hands, one for helping yourself, the other*
>   *for helping others.*
> (https://www.goodreads.com/author/quotes/
> 30932.Sam_Levenson)

Remember to decide for yourself what is important in life, and, when you do, drink deeply of those things. Extraordinary experiences make for an extraordinary life.

Week 21
Healing Hands

The truth is that we are, each of us, perfect, whole, and complete, just as we are; none of us need any fixing. There may be things we want to change in our lives, but even if we never change them, we are still right and perfect just as we are.

Healing Hands. This phrase can be looked at on many levels. It can literally mean medically trained persons stepping in to cure an illness; it can refer to a person who has become a practitioner; or it can mean that special person who stepped into your life when you most needed some assistance. It can be each of us, as we remember that we are here to serve one another with the gift of our lives.

Doctors and nurses provide healing hands when treating illnesses and broken bones. A practice called Reiki, a Japanese technique for stress reduction and relaxation, also promotes healing. It is administered by "laying on hands" and is based on the idea that unseen life force energy flows through us to keep us alive. If one's life force energy is low we are more likely to get sick or feel stress, and if it is high we are more capable of being happy and healthy. It sounds a bit like Religious Science teachings, doesn't it?

According to Wikipedia, the word Reiki is composed of two Japanese words: *Rei,* which means God's wisdom or the higher power, and *Ki,* which is life force energy. So Reiki is actually spiritually guided life force energy. Laying on of hands is a Biblical action; however, there is no Biblical mandate requiring the physical laying on of hands for a particular spiritual ministry. Jesus certainly laid His hands on many of those He healed, but He also healed without laying His hands on people. In fact, there were times when He was nowhere near the vicinity of those He healed. Matthew 8:8 describes Jesus healing the servant of the centurion without going near the centurion's house.

When my first husband's father died, a priest was called in to give last rights. When my father-in-law opened his eyes and saw the priest, he became frantic. The priest told us to lay hands upon him as he prayed, and all of us did so. With just the laying of hands on his body he suddenly became calm. Was there healing in that touch? I certainly think so.

In Religious Science, people are given the opportunity to attend classes in Science of Mind (SOM). Once students have completed the required courses they are eligible to take the next series of classes, which result in being licensed as a practitioner, one who does affirmative prayer for others. They are called *practitioners* because they are trained to heal any aspect of a person's consciousness while knowing and holding the truth that we are each of us perfect, whole, and complete, just as we are. Ernest Holmes imparts this in his *Science of Mind* textbook:

> *The practitioner works within his own mind until he is mentally satisfied, until the whole reaction in his thought causes him to understand that his patient is*

*now healed. This healing is really the action of Spirit
upon the mind of the healer, the active Principle of
truth, goodness and harmony.*

*Since the Divine must hold us as some part of Its
eternal perfection, we are fulfilling our destiny when
we think of ourselves as already Divine and perfect.
To contemplate that Divine Life which is at the very
center of everyman's life—this is the very essence of
mental healing* (409).

Life Coach Mary Morrissey speaks of an illness she had in her early twenties. She was told she had only months to live. Lying in the hospital, she was asked by a chaplain if she could see herself getting better. She said no. The chaplain then asked if Mary would allow her to know it for her. Mary said she would let her do that. Within weeks she was up and healthy and checking out this New Thought spirituality (*Prosperity Plus*—DVD).

What about those special people in our lives who always show up just when we need them, the people who always believe in us, no matter what? My husband, Gary, has a favorite song by Bill Withers called "Grandma's Hands" in which a man remembers the kindness of his grandma.

Do you have people in your life like that right now? People who love you unconditionally? If you do, that's wonderful. If you don't, start finding more time for *you* to be that trusted and caring individual. When you do, you will attract more people just like you.

Reaching out in friendship and service to others is a peaceful thing to do. Reaching out to others also helps bring an end to many illnesses and feelings of depression or sadness. My own mother was a healthy person, living by herself at ninety, giving her friends a lift when she could. Later, when she couldn't get out much, more aches and pains showed up that weren't there when she was more active. Each of our lives is a gift that deserves sharing with others. Don Miguel Ruiz comes from the Toltec teaching.

In his book, *The Fifth Agreement*, he observes that

> *Toltec wisdom arises from the same essential unity*
> *of truth as all the sacred esoteric traditions found*
> *around the world. Though it is not a religion, it*
> *honors all the spiritual masters who have taught on*
> *the earth. While it does embrace spirit, it is most*
> *accurately described as a way of life, distinguished*
> *by the accessibility of happiness and love.* (xii)

This sounds similar to Ernest Holmes' early teachings. When he first began speaking his spiritual philosophy, he was dead against calling it a religion. He would have described his ideas as a way of life. Don Miguel continues,

> *The fifth agreement is ultimately about seeing*
> *your whole reality with the eyes of truth, without*
> *words. The result of practicing the fifth agreement*
> *is the complete acceptance of yourself just the way*
> *you are and the complete acceptance of everybody*
> *else just the way they are. The reward is your eter-*
> *nal happiness.* (xv)

When you can accept yourself as being okay, and you can accept others just the way they are, this is "Truth Expressing."

Healing hands can mean so many things, but when you say to yourself, "I want everyone and everything that crosses my path to be blessed and I want that blessing in return," then you are healing hands in expression.

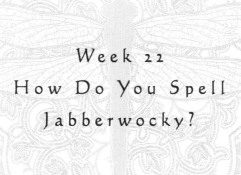

Week 22
How Do You Spell
Jabberwocky?

I am the youngest child in my family. I have two sisters, eight and ten years older than I, and a brother who is seven years older. When I came along, I was like their live baby doll. They taught me everything, including card games, so I could be their fourth for pinochle and canasta. My oldest sister was the one who used me for just about everything she was doing, especially if it concerned schoolwork. When she had to learn a poem by memory, she would teach it to me to help her learn it as well. That's how I learned Lewis Carroll's "The Jabberwocky" from *Through the Looking Glass*,

> *'Twas brillig, and the slithy toves*
> *Did gyre and gimble in the wabe;*
> *All mimsy were the borogoves,*
> *And the mome raths outgrabe.*

And the poem continues with more nonsensical words. As a child I was fascinated with those words and the story of the man who went out to face the Jabberwocky. It was an early lesson in facing fears and overcoming them. I think those early experiences of memorizing lines led to my love of acting and my love of speaking.

The book I'm currently reading, *The Power of Focus* by Jack Canfield, Mark Victor Hansen, and Les Hewitt, takes a look at what helps people lead successful lives. They suggest that resolving unfinished business, counteracting fear, and forgiving and forgetting are contributing factors. They say looking at your faith factor is a good thing as well.

Let's look more closely at that first point, resolving unfinished business. Perhaps there are a few things in your life you haven't dealt with, that you allow to keep simmering or piling up. Perhaps you are holding on to resentment about some wrong you feel was done to you. You have a few choices. You can deny the issues entirely; you can keep them in limbo, periodically bringing them out at night to agonize over; or you can face them head on (*Focus* 157).

Of the three choices, only the last one will ever bring you peace. Take charge and face the issue. If you have a friend or relative who is always asking for something and never seems to lift a helping hand in return, be polite, but be direct. Sometimes when friends or relatives do not have faith in their own success, they will come to you out of fear. Let them know you are always there for them in a pinch, but that making a habit of only taking is not okay. It usually takes a leap of faith to bridge the gap between fear and confidence. Dr. Robert Schuller, the late pastor of the Crystal Cathedral in Garden Grove, California, wrote a poem entitled, "Faith Is Often Called a Leap."

> *Faith is leaping across the gaps*
> *Between the known and the unknown,*
> *The proven and the unproven,*

The actual and the possible,
And the grasp and the reach.
There is always a chasm between where you are
And where you are going—by faith make
The leap forward
What lies ahead? Tomorrow? Next Week?
Next month? Next Year? Beyond this life?
Believe in faith! Believe in God!
Believe in tomorrow!
Take the leap of faith!

(Fubar.com/s/bp1/442)

So how can you overcome fears and uncertainties and start developing positive thinking? Resolve your unfinished business and identify your deeper fears. Address those fears simply by asking, "What can I do to overcome this?"

In the summer of 2007, I took the West B exam to complete my Washington certificate for substitute teaching. I had put this off many times because a math exam was required and I hadn't had math since my sophomore year in high school, over thirty years earlier. I finally took a math book home over the summer and studied for about a month, then took the exam and found it to be a piece of cake. I faced the fear and it disappeared.

In 1999 Nelson Mandela celebrated his eightieth birthday. For almost twenty-six of those years he was confined to a prison cell. During that period his confidence must have been severely tested. It is a tribute to his faith that he ultimately triumphed and went on to be elected to his country's highest office.

Facing fear and challenge is commendable, but what about that resentment you are holding toward someone or something? What happens if you never release that resentment? Medical evidence shows that resentment and fear can lead to a release of stomach acids that can cause physical problems. This sense of disease may be the cause of ulcers and other stomach and intestinal disorders. You may feel there are some things that just can't be forgiven. *The Power of Focus* explains, "No matter how traumatic the experience, to be free, you must forgive. This may not be easy, but it is essential if you want to have peace of mind, and a happier future" (165).

How you do this doesn't matter; it could be a face-to-face confrontation, a phone call, or a letter. Whatever it is, settle the issue within yourself. Let it go and move on. Then, forgive yourself. Silence any negative thoughts of guilt. The past is past. You will never be able to change it. You did what you had to do at the time, and so did your parents (165).

One of the greatest stories of forgiveness and love started many years ago during the Vietnam war. Journalist Patricia Chisholm told the story in Canada's *Maclean's* magazine, February 10, 1997:

> *Nine-year-old Phan Thi Kim Phuc was running through her village when bombs meant for military installations reached her village. She remembers her clothes were burning but she was so afraid that she just kept running. The napalm was like a jelly that stuck to her and caused terrible burns. Nick Ut, a photographer, rushed her to a local hospital. His photograph of the situation won him a Pulitzer Prize.*
>
> *Years later, after years of rehabilitation, Kim, now living in Canada shows an incredible power to forgive. In fall 1996 she participated in a ceremony at the Vietnam Veterans Memorial in Washington, D.C. There she had an unintentional and emotional meeting with Captain John Plummer, the man who ordered the air strike on her village. They sat smiling, holding hands. It was clear that Kim bore no ill will. In this respect Kim is rare. Most people would have held ill will; she chose to avoid reflecting on the war. In her own words she says, "To feel a trace of bitterness even deep inside, is too tiring, too heavy." She is now happily married with a young son to nurture. What an ability to love and forgive.*

This leads right in to the faith factor. We are discovering more and more that having a belief in a personal spirituality is beneficial to human life. Ernest Holmes, in *The Science of Mind*, writes,

> *Man's life, in reality, is spiritual and mental, and until the thought is healed, no form of cure will be permanent. We understand that health is a mental as well as a physical state. We seek to heal men's mentalities, knowing that to the degree in which we are successful, we shall also be healing their bodies. We know, too, that to the degree in which we are able to see a perfect man, he will appear. We feel that the spiritual or real man is perfect and we seek to uncover this perfection which is within every man's life. This is spiritual mind healing.* (190)

So when we face our fears, take care of unfinished business, or let go of old resentments, we are healing our own consciousness. We are all perfect, whole, and complete—but occasionally we forget that, and we need help remembering. May you always recognize the greater wisdom that you are, just as you are, perfect, whole, and complete.

Week 23
Communion with God

Any time of year is perfect for an outing. Travel to the shore, go camping, or just make time to be out in the yard. Why? Outdoors is where we get in touch with our earth, commune with nature, and become more grounded. Ralph Waldo Emerson in his essay "Nature" from *Emerson's Essays* says of the forest,

> *At the gates of the forest, the surprised man of the world is forced to leave his city estimates of great and small, wise and foolish. The knapsack of custom falls off his back with the first step he makes into these precincts. Here is the sanctity which shames our religions, and reality which discredits our heroes. Here we find nature to be the circumstance which dwarfs every other circumstance, and judges like a god all men that come to her.* (381)

Emerson is saying that in nature we are all alike; there is nothing to judge us. In nature we can examine what is real and valuable. Having been a teacher, and having taught an English class or two, I would sometimes have students write in their journals. One of my own wonderful quotes I had my students write about is "Alone in a crowd is lonely; alone by yourself is powerful." This is a simple statement that mirrors Emerson's excerpt from "Nature."

Small talk at parties can at times be amusing, but too often it seems pointless, leaving you feeling awkward and perhaps a little empty. Not so in nature. When you get outdoors, especially when you are enjoying it quietly, the beauty of what is around you speaks volumes.

If you've ever been out on the deck of a ship late at night and watched the endless ocean, or stared at the stars on a cloudless night, you feel the vastness of the Universe. This, too, is communing with nature, or communing with God.

Many religious philosophies would have us meditate, go within to recognize our oneness with God. John Stuart Mill elucidates,

> *Solitude in the sense of being often alone, is essential to any depth of meditation or of character; and solitude in the presence of natural beauty and grandeur is the cradle of thought and aspirations which are not only good for the individual, but which society could ill do without.*
> (whitefiles.org/b4_g/1_free_quotes/)

In Dr. Wayne Dyer's *10 Secrets for Success and Inner Peace,* his fourth law is, "Embrace the Silence." The book tells us that

> *"be still" actually means silence. Mother Teresa described silence and its relationship to God by saying, "God is the friend of silence. See how nature—trees, grass, grow in silence; see the stars, the moon and the sun, how they move in silence . . . . We need silence to be able to touch souls."* (53)

This includes your soul!

Studies have shown that those who meditate are more peaceful and healthy, can lower their blood pressure, are more alert, and have a general sense of well-being. Dyer expresses it this way:

> *The more peaceful you become, the easier you can deflect the negative energies of those you encounter. This is like having an invisible shield around you that nothing can penetrate unless it's at a higher spiritual energy than your shield. A hostile current is greeted with a smile and an inner knowing that this is not your stuff. A person who attempts to bring you into their misery cannot succeed without your agreement. Your meditation practice keeps you immune.* (58)

Are there people you just love to be around because they are so upbeat? Are there others that drain your energy? Sometimes after trying to sway their conversations to something positive and finding it never works, you need to just say, "I'm going to stop spending time with them. Life is too short, and there are so many people that are a joy to be around." Once you establish a regular practice of sitting in silence each day, fewer of those draining situations will come into your life. You become immune to them.

If someone you love bothers you in some way, if something he or she does irritates you, looking at them differently can make you love the person in spite of those little idiosyncrasies. A pastor I knew used to get upset at constantly having to close the cupboard doors her husband left open. One day she decided to simply see this as giving her husband a loving hand in closing the doors, and almost as quickly as she changed her attitude, he began shutting the doors himself. Often, when we expect something to happen, good or "bad," it does. Let's start expecting things to turn out the way we want them to and see what happens. Raymond Charles Barker, author of *The Power of Decision,* takes it one step further:

*When you really know that your inside world is cause
to your outside world and that you have full control
over your consciousness of cause, you have true freedom of both thought and action.* (37)

Another law that Wayne Dyer explains in his *10 Secrets for
Success and Inner Peace* is this:

*Wisdom is avoiding all thoughts that weaken you.
Try this exercise: Stand with one arm stretched out
in front of you and have someone ask you a question.
Lie about the answer while they simultaneously try
to push your arm down. Now have them ask the same
question and tell the truth while they push on your
arm. When you tell the truth it is virtually impossible
to push your arm down without difficulty. When you
lie, it is much easier.* (145)

What does this say about speaking your truth? Did you ever
hear the adage "The truth will set you free"?

In Edgar Allan Poe's "The Tell-Tale Heart," a man murders his
friend and buries him beneath the floorboards of his house.
Friends come over later that evening, among them the sheriff of
the town. As the murderer sits idly chatting with them, he begins
to hear the heartbeat of his dead friend. No one else in the room
appears to hear anything. As he talks, he speaks louder and louder
because he is hearing the heart beating louder and louder. It is the
voice of his conscience. Finally he can contain himself no longer
and admits to the murder; as he does so, the heartbeats stop.

This is a very dramatic example from literature, but think
of all the people who keep a secret out of fear or shame or guilt.
It may take years for them to share their secret, and it may be
painful at first, but sharing an incident with someone else is
sometimes the very solution needed to regain inner peace. What
does Ernest Holmes have to say about the secret for success and
inner peace? He speaks of it in *The Science of Mind Textbook* when
he defines the word *communion*:

Unity . . . agreement . . . We turn to the Father within knowing he will guide us. This is communion. Mental or spiritual contact. (579)

To find outer peace, we must first be at peace within ourselves. When we truly know that goodness and peace is there for the asking, we should simply treat, and then move our feet. Send out the vibrations of affirmative prayer. Ask and you shall receive.

Communing with nature, communing with God—they're the same thing by different names. Like the little tree that plants its shallow roots as a seedling only to deepen them and strengthen them as it branches out into the world, we deepen and strengthen our faith each time we consciously commune with God. It's all about unity, about oneness: One God, one Universe, one Universal Mind. And it is not a secret; it's a spiritual truth readily available to you and me.

Week 24
Candle in the Wind

Most families spend more time together during the summer months. School is out and families go on vacation, finding some quality time to bind them together. It is a time to renew the foundation, to examine the rock. It is a way for the family to stay centered, and by so doing, for each life to become more enhanced.

"Candle in the Wind" was written by Bernie Taupin and Elton John in 1973 to honor the life of Marilyn Monroe; the same words were also used more than forty years ago to describe Janis Joplin. In the years since Monroe's death, other great leaders such as John F. Kennedy and his brother, Robert Kennedy, have died, but just as the lyrics to the song declare, their legends still live on.

What does the phrase, "candle in the wind," refer to? Perhaps it means it takes strength to follow your dreams when there may be interference. It takes strength to keep burning, despite the wind. A candle can easily be blown out, but it also can be relit. "Candle in the wind" may symbolize endurance in the face of adversity.

Which paths have you traveled that met with challenges? Relationships, a road to wellness or sobriety, losing a job and making ends meet until the next new and more fulfilling job comes along, all are trying circumstances at times. Ernest Holmes believed that

> the practice of Science of Mind calls for a positive understanding of the Spirit of Truth, a willingness to let this inner spirit guide us, with the conscious knowledge that "The law of the Lord is perfect." In so far as our thought is in accord with this perfect law, it will accomplish and nothing will hinder it (Science of Mind, 54).

So, when challenges come along we must realize that nothing happens by accident and we must not let those pit stops get in our way. We must remember to be grateful for whatever happens because, in time, we will realize why we had the experience. We must each be the candle in the wind with confidence that our light will remain bright or that occasionally, when it blows out, there is someone standing by with matches. Or perhaps we might move our candle out of the wind entirely. In times of adversity we can stay and be beaten up, or we can learn from the experience, and move on to help someone else encountering similar challenges. Isn't that what each of us strives for, to be a difference maker?

Each of us makes such a positive impact on the lives of others, whether by raising a healthy child, caring for someone who is sick, or listening to someone who just needs an ear. It isn't only the big things in life that make a difference to others. Sometimes the small things matter the most.

I'm sure each of us can think of a time when things didn't go our way, or when we felt shortchanged by another person. But we can also think of a time when someone helped us out in an unexpected way.

A few years ago at a conference in Asilomar, I was standing in line behind a woman who was about 75 cents short of what she needed to pay the bill. I offered to lend her the change, but the cashier said, "No, let me pay it." The cashier then recounted a time when she was pregnant and a little short of the amount she needed to pay a bill and asked the cashier if she could let the amount slide this time. The cashier said, "No, go home and get the extra cash; I'll hold your groceries until you get back." The woman recounting the story said, "I vowed that if I was ever in the same situation, I'd help someone else out." When the customer left and it was my turn in line I remarked how proud I was of her that she learned to help others instead of dumping on them because of how she had been treated.

One of the best secrets for success in life is to remember to return kindness no matter what you are going through. Learn from each incident, no matter how difficult, and move on. When the wind is blowing, pick up the candle and move it out of the wind. Blind studies in hospitals where one group of patients is prayed for and another group is not, found that 90 percent of the people prayed for have had better outcomes than those who were not.

Rev. Judy, one of the co-pastors of my last church, was diagnosed with stage four metabolic colon cancer. When she was diagnosed, she said she didn't want to hear the statistics about what percentage of people in her category survived, or for how long; she just knew whatever the percentage, she was in the group that survived. Since that time she has made her transition to another experience, but she survived for three years when the survival rate is less than half that amount of time.

Our attitude matters—about any condition. Illness, happiness, prosperity, any situation is better when we use the Power of Mind. It's all good, this thing we call life. It is wise to remember that and pass it on to future generations. Always be kind, and remember that what goes around, comes around.

A middle-aged couple found themselves in charge of an elderly parent. After a few months of care they were becoming impatient with the old man. He was starting to be clumsy and quite often broke dishes, and he was very messy. When they could stand it no longer they sat the old man in a corner at a card table during dinnertime and had him eat out of a wooden bowl.

About a week later they found their own son working with some pieces of wood. When they inquired as to what he was doing, he said he was shaping a bowl for them to use when they got older.

Suddenly there was a grasp of reality and at the next meal Grandpa was back at the dinner table with his glass and plate, with food all over him from head to foot, and there were smiles on the faces of his children as they enjoyed and appreciated him and the life he had remaining. (www.inspirationpeak.com)

It is a cycle, isn't it? What we send out, we attract back. Anything we do out of the goodness of our heart is appreciated—big or small, it makes no difference. When it comes to any problem and we say an affirmative prayer, we become the captains of our own souls. Time and Spirit will fill in the details. As Ernest Holmes reminds us, don't dwell on the details; focus on the outcome.

For each of us, life holds many pleasant possibilities and we must focus on positive outcomes. What are you looking for? If it's a job, what are the attributes you want? If it's a relationship, what are the important qualities you desire in a friend or mate? If it's peace, or harmony, or trust, what are you sending out? Like attracts like. In life, each of us is a light making a difference in other lives, so remember this: You can have faith when the flame wavers, you can make a move so your flame burns more steadily, and you can have matches nearby to relight your own flame or be the helping hand when another's flame goes out.

We are the difference makers in our own lives, and quite often in the lives of others.

Week 25
If the Blind Lead the Blind

"Recognize the Richness" is a phrase suggesting that we realize with gratitude the goodness we have in our lives. It is helpful to come to understand that our experiences aren't good or bad, they just are. A major illness may be a wake-up call for someone to slow down and recognize what is important in life. The death of a loved one, particularly at an early age, may wake us up to the gift of life that was shared, even for a brief time, and may be the impetus for sharing gifts with the community in that person's name.

"If the Blind Lead the Blind" is an essay in *Living the Science of Mind* by Ernest Holmes. It clarifies that no man is the ultimate authority on anything, and all we can really live by is our own truth and our own spiritual connection with the Infinite. Dr. Holmes tells us that *in psychological analysis it is believed that if a physician, in analyzing a patient, uncovers in the patient an unconscious hatred for his father, and if the physician had the same aversion for his own father, then the analysis might as well stop right there. This is because the physician is not able to see with clarity a block in another if he has the same type of block in himself.*

In psychological terms this is expressed by saying that wherever there is an emotional bias there will be an intellectual blind spot. This means that we cannot think with truthful clarity about things that we are too emotionally affected by. Jesus understood this, and that is why he said that if the blind lead the blind they will both fall into the ditch. (388)

One experience I endured that is not on the list of "Top Ten Terrific Things That Can Happen to You in a Lifetime" was that of having a cancerous section of my colon removed. When I found out I had cancer I asked a fellow practitioner at my church to do an affirmative prayer treatment for me. She told me afterwards that she had to do an affirmative prayer treatment for herself to get rid of her own fear for me. At first she was too emotionally affected by what I had shared with her. I told her I was never really afraid of having the cancer; I was just asking for a safe journey in my healing.

When I do an affirmative prayer for someone else or for myself, what I am remembering is the truth about them, or the truth about myself—that we are perfect, whole, and complete just as we are. On those occasions when I find myself worrying about finances or health issues, or any problem, I remind myself that I am supported by the Universe in all aspects of my life: I am the peace of God; I am the peace that passes all understanding. When I can let go of the doubt and worry, things always get better. I think of this as letting go and letting God.

The title "If the Blind Lead the Blind" reminds me of the old nursery rhyme from my childhood days: "Three blind mice. See how they run. They all ran after the farmer's wife. She cut off their tails with a carving knife. Have you ever seen such a sight in your life as three blind mice?"

Rhymes.org tells us that the origins of the words to the "Three Blind Mice" rhyme are based in English history. The farmer's wife is the daughter of King Henry VIII, Queen Mary I. Mary was a staunch Catholic, and her violent persecution of Protestants led to the nickname of Bloody Mary. Queen Mary and her husband, King Philip of Spain, possessed massive estates. The three blind mice were three noblemen who adhered to the Protestant faith and were convicted of plotting against the queen. She did not have them dismembered and blinded as inferred in the rhyme, but she did have them burned at the stake!

It is amazing throughout history how many battles have been fought in the name of God. The Crusades are an excellent example. England sent troops into many countries in the name of Christianity. Right here in the United States, during the Civil War, letters were written from both camps talking about how "God was on their side." Now unless God has a split personality, it would be difficult for It to be on both sides. And it's hard to believe that a higher Power in the Universe would be for war. According to Ernest Holmes in *The Science of Mind* textbook,

> *People are prone to say that they alone are right, or their system of thought alone is right. They have not yet gotten a clearance back to the fundamental proposition that God is One, and that every man is an incarnation of the same God. Therefore, intolerance and harshness, unkindness and criticism, coldness and indifference are projected. This is one of the tricks that the mind plays on us.*

*When we understand these things we shall become
more tolerant, more kind, more compassionate, because we shall realize that we are all on the pathway
of evolution, not of Spirit, which is already perfect,
but of the mind which so often is blindly groping in
the dark.* (388)

Science of Mind is a philosophy that allows us to bring more
order to our lives, to be more conscious of what we are feeding
our subjective mind. Positive thoughts attract a positive outcome. We must never look at events in our lives as good or bad,
but just as events that have happened. A divorce may seem horrible at the time we are going through it, but it opens doors for new
experiences, new relationships.

Even the death of a child, while we feel nothing will ever take
away the senselessness of the experience, will often result in good
works. Optimist International, an organization of which I am a
member, supports children's causes. One day this group hosted
the Larsons as guest speakers. They did a presentation about their
son, Cooper, who died at the age of seven from a rare brain cancer.
This young boy loved baseball. Toward the end of his life he was
granted his wish from the Make-a-Wish Foundation to see a
Seattle Mariners baseball game and meet the players on the team.
The Larsons have pictures of Cooper with the players talking to
him at eye level as if he were a peer and not just a little kid. The
parents want to build a baseball park in Cooper's memory, and
people from all over are donating fencing materials, architectural
plans, and concrete work. While there are some minor objections
to the project in the community, they hope to overcome these and
build a stadium for young players, making something good happen in Cooper's memory.

Another family, during the holiday season, was preparing
a meal. After watching her mother cut the ends off of a pot roast
before putting it in the pan, a child asked her mother and grandmother why they did that. The mother said, "I don't know. Mom,
why did you cut the ends off the roast?"

"My mother always did it, so I do it," she said. They both looked at one another and then said, "Go ask Gransy, she's in the living room." The child went in and inquired of her great grandmother why the ends always got cut off the roast, and she said, "I don't know why your mother does it now, but back when I did it, we didn't have a pan big enough to fit it" (www.psychologytoday/the-pot-roast-principle).

Sometimes things get handed down through generations for no rhyme or reason. Before you automatically do something someone else tells you to do, stop and ask why. While teaching Science of Mind classes I have often heard students say they were told in their former church not to come back to Bible study class because they asked too many questions. In my classes, I welcome those questions. I am reminded of a cute billboard sign contest I saw on the Internet. Two churches that face each other across a busy street battled with one another on a weekly basis. One subject for debate: a clash of dogmas as to whether dogs go to heaven.

Our Lady of Martyrs Catholic Church (CC): All Dogs go to Heaven
Beulah Cumberland Presbyterian Church (Pres): Only Humans go to Heaven; read the Bible

CC: God Loves All His Creations, Dogs Included
Pres: Dogs Don't Have Souls; This is Not Open for Debate

CC: Catholic Dogs Go to Heaven, Presbyterian Dogs Can Talk to their Pastor
Pres: Converting to Catholicism Does Not Magically Grant your Dog a Soul

CC: Free Dog Souls with Conversion
Pres: Dogs are Animals; There Aren't Rocks in Heaven

CC: All Rocks go to Heaven
(www.freerepublic.com/focus/chat/2228641)

This is humorous, but the point is that no one knows exactly what happens after this life. I believe I will pass on to another wonderful and new experience, and that's enough for me. I'll concentrate on living the kindest and most productive life I can while I am here.

When we hear, "*This* is what happens to you," isn't that the biggest example of the blind leading the blind? When someone asks you a question and you don't know the answer, is it a good idea to pretend to know? You could choose to say, "Hmm, that's a good question. I'll have to look it up." If you always tell the truth you won't be blindly leading the blind, and you'll never have to remember what you said.

Karen Drucker wrote a great little song called, "N-O is my New Yes." In it, she says, "When I say no, I'm saying yes to myself." If you don't want to do something and you do it anyway, will you enjoy yourself? A close friend will always understand when you give an authentic answer. When you are in a situation because you want to be there, your vision and your participation are genuine and the energy you share is positive.

I had been in Religious Science about a year, doing so much—teaching all day, going to workshops on Saturdays (when I wasn't taking students to speech tournaments), volunteering on Sundays, taking classes or helping with church projects almost every day of the week. I finally realized I was so overwhelmed doing "things" that I lost the time to just sit and be. I was living proof of the philosophy that says, "Ask a busy person to do something and it gets done." But I eventually had to stop and ask myself which areas were the most important to me. I had to learn that it's okay to say, "No, I can't do that at this time."

Life should be a balance, and for me, three things are important: my spiritual life, my means of employment, and my social life. When I give equal time to all these things, I am much more balanced, much more centered, much more at peace. When I am centered and balanced, I have clear vision and am not blinded while too busy doing "things."

Are you too busy? Perhaps you are a parent feeling like you're providing a nonstop taxi service for your kids. Find out if there are other parents who will take turns carpooling one week while you do it the next. At work, perhaps there can be one or two days a week when you can say, "I'm leaving on time today, no matter what." If you think you don't have time for meditation, try meditating when you take a bath. Give yourself a gift and declare, "This is my time to just let go and sink into myself." Whenever there is a challenge in your life, it is good to go inside and allow your inner voice to guide you. This is the wisdom that comes from God. Again from his textbook Ernest Holmes says,

> *The student should take the time every day to see his/her life as he/she wishes it to be, to make a mental picture of his/her ideal. He/she should pass this picture over to the Law and go about his/her business, with a calm assurance that on the inner side of life something is taking place. There should not be any sense of hurry or worry about this, just a calm, peaceful sense of reality. Let the Law work through, and express Itself in, the experience. There should be no idea of compulsion. We do not have to make the Law work; it is Its nature to work. In gladness then, we should make known our desires, and in confidence we should wait upon the Perfect Law to manifest through us.* (272)

Two words in that quote you may or may not know in the Religious Science context: *Law* and *demonstration*. *Law* relates to the idea of cause and effect. We are cause to our own effect. What we think into life comes about. That is the Law, or the thing itself—our thoughts create our reality. *Demonstration* is a manifestation. What we put into the fertile soil of our mind comes about as a manifestation or a demonstration of our thought in motion. If I am doing an affirmative prayer for better working circumstances and a new and better job comes about, that is a demonstration of my affirmative prayer.

So, in the above passage, Holmes is telling us to do affirmative prayer with confidence and know that the Law will provide a demonstration in Divine right order. Don't worry about how or when; just know that Divine right action will happen, that it is so. Allow yourself to be open to the light, the wisdom of God.

There is an allegory written by Plato called, "The Cave." In it there are men who are chained to a wall, facing away from the sun. All they have ever seen are shadows on the wall created by the sun shining on objects that pass behind them. When one man breaks free and sees the world the way it really is, he comes back to tell the others but they are suspicious of this new information that goes against their shadow reality.

When we follow others in any belief without deciding for ourselves what is true and valuable—whether about parenting, moral issues, politics, or religion—we are following blindly. As we center on our spirituality, if we are to live genuinely, we must live solely by *our own truth, our own personal* spiritual connection with the Infinite.

Week 26
I Am a Blessing

Each person on this planet makes a difference in the lives of others; what we say and do in this world does make a difference. No matter how insignificant it may seem to us at times—a smile we offer, the person we wave ahead of us at a stop sign—our kind act may be the one positive moment that happens in someone else's life for that day. Little kindnesses offered from the heart add to the positive vibrations and energy in the Universe.

Be the positive light that makes people want to be around you, and guess what? You will attract back the same. We are so blessed. Try to remember to maintain an attitude of gratitude. When you are thankful, the floodgates are opened for more good to flow your way.

Karen Drucker tells in her book, *Let Go of the Shore*, the story of a song she wrote called, "You Are the Face of God." She had just returned from playing at a wedding—a biker wedding. She hadn't known it was a biker wedding when she said yes to the gig. So instead of two hours of light background music, she played four hours of heavy rock for 150 loud and disorderly bikers. She came home very tired and almost went straight to bed when she saw the blinking light on her answering machine. The call was from the minister of her church where she was music director, asking if she could write a five-minute song on forgiveness for her talk the next day. Tired from the day, she mumbled a few ungod-like words and went to bed.

The next morning she sat at the piano with a few words that had been e-mailed to her as a start for the song, and slowly, "You Are the Face of God" came out. The message behind the song is that no matter who you encounter, if you can honestly say, "You are the face of God, you are a part of me," then you are testifying to our oneness and being a positive light in the world (76).

Many people are going through difficult times. It's important to realize that they are going *through* them—they aren't permanently stuck, and they don't need to stop and have a pity party. When a challenge presents itself to me, I often take time to seriously examine the problem. I might say, "Hmmm, this is interesting. I wonder why I am having this experience?" but behind it all I understand that I go through *everything* in my life on purpose. There will always be some incident in the challenge I can grow from. I will look back and understand that the problem was a catalyst for something new and improved in my life. It may even be that when someone else goes through the same challenge, I will be there to empathize and show the way through and out.

Rev. Jeanette Keil was a dear friend. She helped people move through challenges with her book, *Invitation to Wellness,* about people experiencing different forms of mental illness. Bipolar episodes in her own life started showing up when she was in college. She went on to become a Religious Science minister, a psychologist, and a great example, proving that such challenges don't have to inhibit one's ability to function effectively in society. The insights in her book are inspiring.

So often our ability to listen to someone else without advising, without judgment, is the greatest gift we can bestow. We become a blessing to that person and when they feel blessed, the floodgates are opened for more goodness.

I recently started to feel overwhelmed. I had a talk to write, a class to prepare, three tutoring sessions needing materials, a "Wise Woman" flyer to produce, and an Optimist Oratorical contest to organize. I was on the verge of mental overload when suddenly I said, "No, don't panic; be calm about this. God never gives me more than I can handle. What do I need to do tonight? Everything will get done, and I can do it easily. What do I need to do now, in this moment?"

When I let go of the fear, when I released the worry, everything flowed smoothly. I surrendered to the Divine Power within me to allow everything to get done in perfect right order. The next morning I woke up before the alarm, feeling fresh and ready to go. I had the gift of an extra hour-and-a-half to accomplish one more task. Being relaxed allowed my time management skills to kick in smoothly and effortlessly. Have the faith to let go and let God. Make that new decision and flow with it. Know that as it says in the Bible, Matthew 19:26, "With God, all things are possible."

What we say and do in this world makes a difference. Once we embody the inspiration that with God all things are possible, we truly comprehend what affirmative prayer is all about. Develop the habit of remembering to know that everything *always* works out for the best, and that you really can remain calm in the face of anything that occurs. The more you practice remembering, the easier it becomes. That is a connection with true meaning. And that is how you come to know what a blessing you are.

Week 27
In the Beginning
There Was Love

Think back for a moment to the first time you fell in love. Do you remember how quickly your heart beat whenever you saw the object of your affection? Perhaps you associate certain smells or a song with that first love.

In the beginning there was love. The word love can bring to mind a variety of loving relationships: the romantic love between two people, the love of parents for a child, or the love one has for a treasured pet. It can also mean the spiritual love we experience toward a greater power that created us. Whatever measure of love we feel, it is always magnified when we recognize the love within ourselves—when we can honestly say, "I am loved, lovable, and loving" and mean it. When we know the love that comes from within, all the other loves in our lives transpire more vividly and instinctively. *The Science of Mind* textbook glossary defines love as

> *the self-givingness of the Spirit through the desire of life to express Itself in terms of creation. Emerson tells us that Love is a synonym for God. We are also told in the New Testament that "He that loveth not, knoweth not God; for God is love." Love is free from condemnation, even as it is free from fear. Love is a cosmic force whose sweep is irresistible.* (608)

The textbook by Ernest Holmes says, "Love is spontaneous; Law is impersonal . . . . Love points the way and Law makes the way possible" (43). Let's look closer at some of those definitions and see how love is not only a beginning, but also a life journey.

Love is the self-givingness of the Spirit through the desire of Life to express Itself in terms of creation. This has to do with our own consciousness and the Law of cause and effect. Everything in our lives comes about by our own thinking. If we have an idea and can truly embody it, we can achieve what we conceive. Have you ever had that gut feeling in a job interview that everything was going well and you just knew you were going to get the job? Whether you get the job or not has much to do with the mental attitude you have about receiving it. When you are sure of yourself, confidence emanates from you. All of it starts with Spirit, the true desire to be or have something. The thought occurs to change jobs, the ideas come as to what to do to prepare for and apply for another job, and our subconscious works on that desire. When it comes about, it has expressed itself in terms of creation.

Love is free from condemnation, even as it is free from fear. I think of this statement as being particularly true when I think of the love that a parent has for a child. So many times when a child does something that causes him to be in great danger—perhaps taking a car without permission and getting into an accident—parents are never as concerned about the damage to the car as they are about their child's safety.

Very often when a teenage girl becomes pregnant, she *thinks* her parents will disown her, and, actually they become her best advocate. Sharing any situation with a parent takes the burden off one person and shares it with another. When love is free from condemnation, it is unconditional.

Real love is also free from fear. Love is knowing in your heart that good things happen for people, and it allows you to follow your dreams without the fear of failure. How many times in our lives have we let fear get in the way of doing something? The pill bug as he crawls along may curl up into a ball for a short time, but he doesn't stay that way. He eventually opens himself up to a new possibility.

Ray Bradbury has a story called "The Whole Town's Sleeping" in *Dandelion Wine* about a young girl walking home alone late at night. She is walking down a ravine with hundreds of steps when she hears footsteps following her. She takes two steps; she hears two echoes. She takes three; she hears three more. She is convinced someone is following her. She races home and fumbles for her key to the front door. Shakily she turns the lock, goes inside, secures the deadbolt and stands panting in relief. The last line to the story is, "Behind her in the living room, someone cleared his throat." The point is that we can be afraid of something all our lives, and it may actually exist as in this story but more often does not. We must overcome our fears and follow our passion, follow our love.

What about romantic love? *Spiritual Fitness* by Caroline Reynolds is a wonderful book that I encourage you to read. The author talks about the three laws of successful relationships: self-love, respect, and freedom. She says of self-love, "It's impossible for you to connect with someone else's heart if you haven't connected first with your own." In other words you must first know that you are loved, loveable and loving. You must be comfortable in your own skin. This is true for romantic love and it is true for friendship.

On respect, Reynolds comments, "Part of the job of respecting your partner is to allow them to go at their own pace and learn their own lessons for themselves." This is true for our partners, our friends and our children. Part of life is learning things for ourselves. "For your relationship to thrive," she goes on to say, "you must both allow each other the space to grow and shine as individual beings on a path of evolution." (76-77)

Reynolds points out that often we become jealous of our loved ones for the very reason that attracted us to them in the first place—flirting, for example. In reality, when we allow the space for loved ones to express themselves, we can celebrate and admire their strengths and we set each other free to blossom.

"Love is spontaneous, Law is impersonal," said Ernest Holmes. Those ideas that we have to do or be something different from our present experience come from Spirit. They are love, or Spirit, expressing. Our thoughts about these ideas are subject to the cosmic Law of cause and effect as the God-force around us does not play favorites; it gives us exactly what we believe.

If I want to sing or dance but I let my negative voice tell me it's not possible, that is exactly what will happen—I won't be able to sing or dance. The reverse is also true. If I want to sing or dance, and I take voice lessons, or go to a dance class, and I follow through with those ideas, believing in my own ability, then that is also true; I *can* sing and dance. The Law of cause and effect works on the principle that Ernest Holmes so wisely referred to in the Bible: "It is done unto you as you believe."

"Love points the way, and Law makes the way possible" is another way to say the same thing. We get our ideas from Spirit, and by planting those ideas into our subconscious minds, the Law of cause and effect demonstrates those ideas in form: new jobs, relationships, better health and finances. If things are not going the way you wish, the solution is to "Change your thinking and change your life."

In the beginning there was love: God's creative energy about us and in us. This creative Intelligence is with us as we progress on our journey of life. We can allow this Law of God to work around us, in us, and through us, just as we allow the law of gravity to work—we do not question, we let it flow. We plant our ideas into Mind and confidently let go and let God. And so it is!

Week 28
Life Is a Dance

A dance between two people has its magic moments when all is in sync. Things get awkward when both dancers try to lead, and they don't get anywhere when both try to follow with no one leading. The magic comes when they dance in time to the music, trusting themselves and each other.

Life is like a dance, with magic showing up when you trust where life will lead you; when you truly believe God is good, and you know you are supported by Spirit. When you absolutely believe life unfolds exactly as it should, then you are trusting where life leads you. If your affirmative prayer each day is for the highest and best in your life, that the right people will be in the right place to accommodate right action in your life, then that is what will happen. Life is a dance, and your partner is Spirit.

When you are trapped in traffic on the highway, what can you do to keep from feeding that idea of stuckness? You can choose to remember times when the traffic flow was smooth, like a dance, cars merging and changing lanes with synchronicity, like a weaving in space, timed to perfection, until the traffic jam passes. If you believe every day that Spirit is guiding you, even when life's little detours show up on your path, what do you think your life would be like?

Devastating events have happened to all of us. I've been through a divorce and survived surgical removal of a cancerous tumor. Neither experience was on my Top Ten List. You also have been through your own misfortunes, but you grew stronger as a result. We all have. We learn compassion, perhaps embrace a new religious philosophy, and weeks or months or years later, we realize certain events had to take place in order for our lives to be as they are today. Life is a dance. Sometimes we are abruptly aware of the steps, and other times we flow naturally with the rhythm of life.

The Moses Code is a wonderful movie about the power of attraction and how we can contribute to the peaceful vibrations of the planet. An actor, inspired by the events of 9/11, started a traveling troop to share positive, constructive, creative ideas for helping each other and the planet. He and a friend had visited New York City shortly after the Twin Towers collapsed. He said as he came in to the city he had a God moment when everything around him moved in slow motion. He saw everyone helping each other, connected, a unity of people working in harmony. He found himself crying, not due to the horror of the aftermath, but to the concept of everyone working together for a common cause. He knew somehow he would do something as a result of this disaster.

At the opening of the movie, we see several religious leaders, including Michael Beckwith and Mary Morrissey, talking about the phrasing of the term, "I Am That I Am." The consensus was that it is a realization of the self, and that the phrase should really be saying, "I Am That, I Am." So when you want to be more prosperous, involved in a meaningful relationship, healthier, or more fit you would say, "I Am Healthy, I Am" or, "I Am Financially Fit, I Am."

I know the Universe supports me, as the Universe supports us all. I know there is more than enough for every person on earth to prosper. When I know this and can let go and let God, then it is so. My new mantra for each morning is *I gratefully accept all the riches life has to offer.* Say this out loud. Say it several times over the next few days and weeks. *I gratefully accept all the riches life has to offer.* Now you're dancing.

Week 29
It Can Move Mountains

Faith can move mountains. Aligning ourselves with Spirit and watching the goodness that abounds is a wonderful experience. Any God quality you imagine—peace, love, beauty, any attribute—must first be acknowledged and celebrated within yourself before you can find and appreciate it in others.

"It Can Move Mountains" comes from *Joyous Freedom Journal*, by Petra Weldes and Christian Sorenson. The God quality it refers to is love.

> *More powerful than the waves of the ocean, the winds of the sky, or the shifting of the earth is Love. Love is the greatest avenue of Divine Expression that you can know. It can move mountains, transmute pain into joy, scarcity into abundance, and sickness*

into health. It will take the dim, dreary, down-and-out point of view on life and brighten the horizon with Infinite choices, enticing relationships, and fulfilling days. (February 26)

When I first moved into my new condo after my divorce some fifteen years ago, I experienced a blessing I did not at first recognize as a blessing. I experienced, for the first time in my life, living alone. I would come home to an almost empty house—my dog Scooby was there, but no humans. I went to bed at night with no one but the dog there with me. Fortunately, I had enrolled in classes at church and was learning about the concept of loving myself first before being truly ready to love others. I found that I began to love the solitude. Then, when I finally knew I was loved, lovable, and loving, Gary, my second husband, walked into my life.

What I also discovered was how to become a joyous and loving contributor to the community around me. Opportunities abound to volunteer at a local school or hospital, or the Red Cross—gleaning fruits and vegetables for a neighborhood food bank, or seeing what your friends and family might need a hand with. When you are in service to others it is very hard to be down on yourself.

The first Special Olympics International Summer Games were held in Chicago in 1968, spearheaded by Eunice Kennedy Shriver in honor of her sister, Rosemary Kennedy. A physical education teacher in the Chicago Park District, Anne McGlone Burke, had presented to Shriver the idea of providing games for children with special needs. With a grant from the JFK Foundation, the games became a reality and have continued for over forty years.

Each one of us makes a difference in the lives of other people. Once we are aware of what our positive attitude can do for others, we can consciously pass that attitude on. When negativity crosses our paths we simply make the choice to give it a new positive face.

There is a story, "A Simple Gesture" by Walter W. Schlatter, in *Chicken Soup for the Soul* where a young man, Mark, was attending a new school and at the end of the day turned from his locker and dropped all his books. Several people laughed at him and went on their way, but one young man, Bill, stopped and helped him get his books together and then in talking, they discovered they lived near one another. Bill invited Mark in for a Coke and they became fast friends. Eventually as Mark neared graduation he thanked Bobby for befriending him on that day in junior high when he had dropped his books. It was then he shared that he had been planning on committing suicide and was cleaning his locker out; in fact, he had already written a farewell note when they met. You never know just how much of a difference you can make in someone's life, simply by being friendly (35).

Week 30
Looking Through a New Lens

When a window is clean, we can see through it. When we are open and honest with each other, we see each other more clearly. And when this happens, the world seems like a happier, safer place.

"Looking through a new lens"–when I first saw this phrase, I was immediately thrown back to my childhood days. Do you remember as a child watching someone focus sunlight through a magnifying glass on a pile of leaves or dried grass? Perhaps you tried it yourself. I was amazed at the power focused light could have. That magnifying glass was a lens, and is a great analogy for the power we have when we connect with the Power of God.

"See Yourself Through a New Lens," is a chapter in Wayne Dyer's book, *Excuses Be Gone*. He contends that if you've always done something the same way, it is quite often hard to change, but it is never impossible. We have the power to change whatever it is we want to change. Here are Dyer's words:

I invite you to try on a new lens that lets you access your false self with its ton of excuses and its belief in limitations. As it edges God out, your false self forces you to part with ideas that prove you're a spiritual being having a temporary experience. Ego gives you a rationale for creating the rationalizations and justifications that eventually direct your life. They become so embedded in what social scientists call the subconscious that your habitual mind turns into an excuse machine. (24)

Just because something in your life appears to be set in stone doesn't mean it has to be a permanent reality. There are countless stories of people who live through catastrophic health challenges and change their whole approach to life. People with weight issues that lead to coronary problems have changed old eating and exercise habits to shed pounds. Older people with sedentary lives, sometimes near death, have begun walking, and eventually even running, to add productive years to their lives. It all begins with a mindset.

Dyer in *Excuses Be Gone,* tells the story of a monk who lived his life at the top of a coconut tree. He was calm and serene and never seemed to have a care in the world. As people passed they would talk to the monk and realize he gave sound advice and guidance. One day the king sought out the monk and said to him, "Tell me how I can succeed in life." The monk did not immediately answer and at first the king thought the monk did not hear him, so he asked a little louder, "What is the secret to success in life?" Still the monk was silent. After a few more minutes he finally replied, "The secret to success in life is to do good things and avoid doing bad things." The king was annoyed and said, "That is of no use to me. That is so obvious. I heard that when I was three years old." To that the monk replied, "It is one thing to hear it; it is another thing to keep doing it." (30-31)

Part of being transparent is remembering and exemplifying the good in life: kindness, love, joy, wisdom . . . and continually practicing positivity. For many of us, it is easy to be positive about one aspect of life, while another area may not be so trouble-free. Fortunately, I have always had a cheery, positive attitude about life in general. If I wake up and I'm not happy, I wonder what's going on.

When I first discovered the Religious Science philosophy I found it was easy to think of myself as peaceful and kind, but much harder to think of myself as someone who succeeded in relationships or had any level of prosperity consciousness. I put effort into seeing myself as loved, loveable, and loving. As I mentioned earlier, I had just gone through a divorce, was living in a condo by myself, and I had to ask myself, "What do I enjoy doing?" Then I had to go out and do it alone if I couldn't find someone to do it with me. I grew to realize that if I wanted to do something I liked and I met someone doing the same, that would be grand, but if not, at least I gave myself the gift of doing something I enjoyed.

Work on my financial state required an attitude change as well. I needed to shift my thinking and appreciate how fortunate I was to be able to pay my bills, and be thankful that people trusted me enough to let me use credit when needed. I started writing TYG (Thank You God) on all my checks before I sent them off. When I felt genuine gratitude for every aspect of my world, things changed. I was looking at life through a positive lens.

Sometimes, particularly in relationships, we become trapped by a sense of guilt. Terry Cole-Whittaker in her book *What You Think of Me Is None of My Business* says there are two kinds of guilt: real guilt and false guilt. False guilt is laid upon you by others in an effort to control you. A mother might say to her son, "Go out and have a good time. Don't think about me here, all alone; I can always watch television." The son goes out, but in the back of his mind is, "Gee, Mom's all alone." Dr. Cole-Whittaker recounts,

Real guilt occurs when you suppress another person mentally, physically or spiritually; when you deny other persons the support they need to believe in themselves. Webster's defines this as, "the fact of having done wrong or committed an offense." In the example of the parent and child, the parent was acting out of real guilt, while the child was acting out of false guilt. (18)

The parent here was mentally suppressing the son's ability to have a good time. The son accepted the false guilt that was laid upon him. We suffer real guilt when we are the suppressors, and false guilt when we are suppressed. Terry continues,

True relationship must come from the position of, "I love and support you to be all that you are and all that you are not. I love and support myself to be all that I am and all that I am not. We are in this relationship because we choose to be and not because we have to be. I will not harm you or myself. Each of us is capable of being, doing and having what we want. Each releases the other from the responsibility of being his or her source and the provider of happiness and wellbeing. We acknowledge that God is the source; people are the avenues. Yes, from time to time when I'm giving myself the permission to love myself, it may appear to you that you are the one who has showered me with love feelings. The reality is that the love feelings I feel when I am with you come out of me." (18)

In a relationship when there is guilt or any other type of problem, we need to focus the lens and realize that our happiness or unhappiness comes from within. Problems exist because we allow them to exist. In any challenge, talk about it, have the courage to see with clearer vision, release what needs to be released, and change what can be changed, or, set the lenses down.

When we speak of doing an affirmative prayer treatment, we recognize the Divine Intelligence of God, and our connection with It. We place into Mind what we want to come about; we give thanks and then let it go. When it manifests, we have a demonstration. Ernest Holmes defines a demonstration in his *Science of Mind* textbook:

> To demonstrate means to prove, to exemplify, to manifest, to bring forth, to project into our experience something that is better than what we had yesterday . . . less pain, less unhappiness, less poverty, less misery, more good . . . this is what is meant by a demonstration. (314)

Making the decision to change what is not working in our lives may take a slight adjustment, or even a more dramatic shift, but we have such a feeling of happiness and peace when we look at problems through a new lens.

There is a story in Gary Chapman's book *The Five Love Languages* called "Conversation in a Mill Town," about a couple that have been married for about five years. They are finding it hard to see things they love about each other any more, and since they know Chapman had written a book on relationships, they go to him for some counseling. During the course of conversation Chapman asks what things drew them together initially, and the wife explains that they used to do things together and help each other out. He would come over to her house in the afternoon, help her with projects, stay for dinner and then help her with the dishes. He said he enjoyed helping her. She says now that they are married he never helps around the house. The husband responds by saying that when he was growing up, his father never helped with anything, and that's how he sees married life. When he realizes his patterns are based on childhood memories he's able to realize he is not his old habits. Then he claims she never wants him to go fishing or hunting by himself, and she lets him know that as long as he does some things with her, those trips are not a problem (92-98).

These two individuals needed to learn they could share the lens sometimes and look through it independently as well. When there are two candles burning separately on the altar during a wedding ceremony and one unlit candle in the center, a newly married couple together will take the lit candles and light the center candle as a symbol of the unity they share; but they then replace their lighted candles in their original holders to represent their ongoing personal independence within their marriage.

Many people would say that when you embrace Science of Mind you are looking at God through a new lens. It is certainly a different lens from the one my parents looked through. When I visited a Religious Science church for the first time, I just knew I finally had the right prescription for me. It is my belief that every person has a spirituality unique to him or her, so we all look at life through a different lens. Science of Mind is difficult for some people to embrace because you can no longer be a victim. There suddenly becomes no one to blame and nobody else to solve your problems. The Power is within, and that's where you connect with God. Ernest Holmes, in the textbook, assures that

> with God all things are possible. We must know this, and this Power of God must be hooked up with our thought, with what we are doing. Energy unconnected does nothing, it is only when it is used, properly directed, that it accomplishes things. (315)

This brings us back to the idea of the magnifying glass and the focused lens. We have the Power to connect our thoughts with the Mind of God and accomplish anything we set our minds to accomplish. We have the power to change whatever it is we want to change. The truth is that we are, each of us, perfect, whole, and complete, just as we are.

Week 31
Listen to the Whisperer

Have you ever suddenly had that intuitive feeling that something was wrong—or right—and then spontaneously acted on it? Maybe it involved another person, or it allowed you to make a good choice about a career move. Where did that voice of inspiration come from?

The Awesome Power of God surrounds us when we listen to the whisperer. Listening to the whisperer is listening to that still small voice within, the voice of God, that Divine inspiration that resides within each of us.

A wonderful movie, *The Horse Whisperer,* is about two girls who go horseback riding in winter and are hit by a skidding truck on an icy road. One horse and child survive the accident, but are in critical condition. The mother seeks the assistance of a man in Montana who communicates with horses and asks him to help heal her daughter and her horse. In their initial meeting, the man sits silently with the horse through those first moments of caution and fear. Ultimately, they achieve a total rapport with each other and the healing takes place.

Isn't it true when we are going through something difficult that the best gift is quite often someone who will simply listen to us without speaking, without giving advice, just being present, really hearing what we need to say? In his book *A New Earth,* Eckhart Tolle speaks of a neighbor who came to his door one evening, frantic. She came in, spent about an hour telling of her troubles, and then left, profusely thanking her host. Eckhart had done nothing other than just listen. The next day, the neighbor said to him, "I don't know what you did for me last night, but it was so helpful. Thank you" (175-176).

As I learned more about Science of Mind, about going inside my own soul and communing with God, I learned to trust that still small voice within me, that intuition, that inspiration that comes from the Divine. Wayne Dyer in his book *Getting in the Gap* likens the need for meditation to the whitecaps on the ocean. There is always turmoil on the surface of the ocean, but when you go below, when you go deep, the water is calm. When you meditate, you rid yourself of that surface turmoil (7).

There are many ways to meditate, and Patrick Harbula describes one in his wonderful book *The Magic of the Soul,* which also includes a CD that provides some excellent guided meditations. He talks of a form of meditation called Zen Tennis. It is a type of walking meditation and can be applied to any sport or activity. He gives the example of a tennis game. He says to get yourself so involved in the mechanics of the game that no other thought enters your mind. Think about the ball as it comes toward you; see the lines on the ball, the strings in your racket and how they meet. Be aware of the smells around you, perhaps the roses in the air, and the music or birds or whatever sounds you hear. Observe the cracks in the concrete in the ground around you. Become so immersed in the whole aspect of the game that all other thoughts are crowded out (156).

For me that level of concentration comes when I build a puzzle or spend time at the gym lifting weights. I let all idle thoughts slip away and become absorbed in the moment. At night, when I clear my mind to meditate and thoughts are racing, I group all my thoughts about the events of the day into one category, all my thoughts about family into another, and I concentrate on the empty space between the two. A teenage girl in one of my classes said she has learned to place the events of the day on an imaginary large computer screen, and then she uses the minimize key to place them on the bottom of the screen, one by one.

Why do we meditate? To get closer to God, to calm ourselves, to lower our blood pressure, and to feel more centered and rested. God's Power is awesome and always available to us. We need only to remember to go inside and listen to that still small voice—the voice of the Creative Intelligence of God whispering to us. When something is not working in our lives and we go within, very often the right idea shows up or we are suddenly inspired and know the perfect person to go to for help. When we go within, we remember to do prayer treatment and remind ourselves about the truth of ourselves, that we are perfect, whole, and complete, with no disease. We remember to *know* we have more than enough for our wants and needs, and that goodness flows to us and is stored in the reservoir of our consciousness. When we remember this, it will be so, because what we think about comes about.

Week 32
Magnetic Thoughts

Just as the buds on the dogwood tree in my front yard have the intention of blooming each spring, so do we have that same opportunity to blossom as we open our minds to new ideas and new possibilities.

"My Thoughts Are Like Powerful Magnets" reads the front of a Law of Attraction card from a deck by Esther and Jerry Hicks. The flip side of the card reads,

> *Your thoughts are powerful, attractive magnets attracting to themselves, and you attract thoughts to you, by giving your attention to them. Those who speak most of prosperity have it, and those who speak most of sickness or poverty have it. It is Law. It can be no other way.*

I remember hearing when I was young, "I'm rubber and you're glue; whatever you say bounces off me and sticks to you," and "It takes one to know one," and "What goes around comes around." All of these sayings had negative connotations at the time, but it's amazing how true that youthful wisdom was.

Our thoughts are magnetic and attract into our lives whatever we focus on. If we send out anger and judgment, that is what is reflected back to us. If we expect a certain situation to be difficult, it becomes difficult. If we know everything will run smoothly and perfectly, guess what? That is exactly what happens. Ernest Holmes teaches in his *Science of Mind* textbook, "What we shall attract will depend upon that on which our thoughts dwell" (294).

If you say, "Oh, this always happens to me," or "I always get a cold in winter," or "I never have enough money for extra things," the Universe in return says, "Yes you're right." One of my students kept saying, "I want a big screen TV. I don't have one and I want one," until his wife reminded him, "Honey, that musician friend of yours sent you a check for $500 for helping him be successful in the industry." He had put into Mind that he wanted the TV, and the money showed up for it. Dr. Holmes goes on to tell us,

Every person is surrounded by a thought atmosphere. This mental atmosphere is the direct result of his conscious and unconscious thought, which, in its turn, becomes the direct reason for, and cause of, that which comes into his life.

As God's thoughts make worlds, and people them with living things, so our thought makes our world and peoples it with our experiences. By the activity of our thought, things come into our life and we are limited only because we have not known the Truth. (294)

Can you think of something that has come into your life because you just knew it would happen? I knew when I went to Indianapolis for my aunt's memorial service that my sister would need to be in control (a take-charge trait found in many of us). It turned out to be true, but my experience with her was different from other visits because this time I let her be in charge without letting it become a negative encounter. I simply asked how I could be of help. Because I have that same desire to be in charge at times, a year ago I would have argued that my ideas might have been better. This time I let go and let God. And it was a lovely memorial.

Isn't it interesting how we can learn so much when we allow ourselves to be in the moment and go with the flow? When we, as friends and family, help each other out and offer our gifts to each other, we create such loving situations. A wonderful, magnetic thought is expressed so beautifully in the Bible: *Do unto others as you would have them do unto you.* This is an extension of the idea of magnetic thoughts. The energy we are sending out, we are getting back. Walter Starke, in *It's All God,* states,

> *Thought is energy. It takes energy to think. We might be frightened that we might run out of energy except for the fact that each human being is made up of trillions upon trillions of atoms and each atom potentially has enough energy to light the world. When we absorb that idea and become consciously aware that we are powerhouses of pure energy, we need no longer "disempower" ourselves. We begin to realize how much more we are capable of accomplishing than we have previously realized.* (178)

When we recognize this, it behooves us to use that power constructively, to be aware of our families, neighbors, community, and world, and how we can make a positive difference in them. Starke goes on:

> *Consciousness is energy and we are consciousness. When that is realized, a new morality comes into play based on how we use our energy or spirit. Do we use it to heal or destroy? Do we allow our lips to*

energize unloving projections or do we transform
appearances by expressing ourselves as the energy
of Love? (179)

The energy of love, peace, harmony, wisdom . . . isn't it wonderful when we think about what kind of positive energy we are sending out? Jesus said the two most important commandments are Love God, and Do unto others as you would have them do unto you.

But what happens when you do kindly unto others and they don't respond in the same manner? A sign on the wall of Mother Teresa's children's home in Calcutta reminds us what we should do in these instances:

ANYWAY

People are unreasonable, illogical, self-centered
. . . love them anyway.
If you do good, people will accuse you of selfish, ulterior motives
. . . do good anyway.
If you are successful, you win false friends and true enemies
. . . be successful anyway.
The good you do today may be forgotten tomorrow
. . . do good anyway.
Honesty and frankness will make you vulnerable
. . . be honest and frank anyway.
People love underdogs but follow only top dogs
. . . follow some underdog anyway.
What you spend years building may be destroyed overnight
. . . build anyway.
People really need help but may attack you if you try to help
. . . help people anyway.
If you give the world the best you have, you may get kicked in the teeth
. . . but give the world the best you have
. . . ANYWAY

(Kent M. Keith, "Paradoxical Commandments")

Week 33
Mirror Image

Ernest Holmes says in his *Science of Mind* textbook, "Life is a mirror and will reflect back to the thinker what he thinks into it" (322).

Did you ever have a day where things weren't going your way, or maybe a day when absolutely everything went beautifully? Life has a way of reflecting back to you what you think into it. Thoughts create your reality. Life has conveniently surrounded us with reflective surfaces: Everybody and everything is reflecting back to us some thought, feeling, or attitude that we are carrying around. To use the mirror effectively requires paying attention to what our mind thinks it sees.

Don Miguel Ruiz wrote a wonderful book, *The Four Agreements,* which are: 1) Be impeccable with your word; 2) Don't take anything personally; 3) Don't make assumptions; and 4) Always do your best. When paying attention to what your mind thinks it sees, try to remain aware of 2 and 3 (25, 47, 63, 75).

Don't take anything personally. Do you know someone who needs time to mellow out after he comes home from work? Or maybe it's you who needs some downtime at the end of the day. Aren't there moments when you don't want to be distracted and just need uninterrupted quiet? If you don't get the alone-time you need, do words sometimes escape from your mouth that might not otherwise be said? Have you ever received criticism that you don't necessarily agree with? Someone may not like your taste in music, but does it mean she doesn't like you? Don't take *anything* personally.

Don't make assumptions. A friend emailed me a story about a woman who was at her veterinarian's office to have her dog's shots updated when in walked a woman with a cat in the most deplorable condition—it was raggedy and matted and filthy and looked as if it was covered in fleas. The woman with the dog turned slightly away, immediately making judgments about the woman. *How could she be so inconsiderate toward a living creature?* She went on and on in her mind, berating the woman for her carelessness. After a few minutes the woman with the cat said, "I found this cat in the alley. I spent about a half-hour coaxing her to come out and be fed. My daughter's cat was run over by a car last week, and so I felt I had to do something. When I called the vet he said to bring her in and he'd treat her." To use the mirror effectively requires paying attention to what our mind thinks it sees. Don't make assumptions. Whenever your mind tells you something about what your eyes see, such as, "She is so beautiful," or, "He is being so sarcastic," try to come up with at least three examples of how this is also true of you. How are you beautiful? How are you sarcastic? This is a way to begin to develop a consciousness of wholeness.

One time while my mother was visiting with me, she bought some placemats to take back home to my sister. After the visit

I flew back with my mother to New Mexico and we were both surprised to find that while my mother was away, my sister had landscaped my mother's front yard. My mother studied the yard and knew right away it was not the way she would have done it. Then my mother showed my sister the placemats, and they were not the color she would have picked out. Each was looking for appreciation from the other, which neither received to their satisfaction. Sometimes, what you feel you are lacking in a relationship is the same lack the other person feels.

From time to time we must go beyond surface appearances. Children with undiagnosed learning disabilities may be struggling as hard as they can and yet be accused by teachers of being lazy. Someone you may think of as being standoffish or stuck-up may actually be shy or afraid of people. What is the illusion and what is the reality? Ernest Holmes tells us in *The Science of Mind* textbook,

> *Wherever the image of thought is set, there the Power to create resides. "God if thou seest God, Dust if thou seest dust." Can we see good where evil appears to be? Then we can remove the evil. When we bring a lamp into a darkened room, where does the darkness go? The darkness neither came nor did it go, anywhere. It never was a thing of itself, merely a condition. And we have power over conditions.*

> *The light is greater than the darkness nor has the darkness any power over the light. The darkness is the great denial of the light but it really did not deny the light for where the light was the darkness was not. By merely bringing in the light the darkness vanished into its native nothingness. This is the power of Reality over seeming opposition or apparent separation.*

The relationship between the individual and the Universal Mind is one of reflection. That is, what we imagine for ourselves, It imagines for us. (410)

Did you ever have an argument with someone in your family and say to yourself, *Oh, why is he/she so stubborn?* Just as much as you want something your way, they may want it to be their way. So who is the stubborn one?

I lived with my mother for six months after I was divorced, and she taught me a very valuable lesson. She taught me to be able to say, "I never thought of it that way." When we were arguing over something we both felt strongly about, I discovered it was just as easy for me to say, "I never thought about it that way before," and we could then go on to discuss something more agreeable.

Life is a mirror image because life is about the power of attraction. What we are sending out is what we are receiving back. The face of God is in every person and situation we encounter. When we treat for something, it is the mirror image that manifests. Our manifested demonstrations are always reflections of our thoughts, even in those times when we may not notice the likeness because it shows up differently than we had imagined.

Have you ever fully grasped the realization that there are no limitations upon you except those you put upon yourself? Your limitations are solely your creation, those to which you agree. Nothing in the entire world can set you free from limited conditions as long as you hold those restrictions in mind. You must first perceive yourself to be free before you can expect to be free from what seems like an outer condition that limits or binds you. You can free yourself from limitation only through knowing Truth and letting it set you free. You must free yourself of all belief that any person or thing can interfere with your perfect freedom or fullest expression. You need to erase from your mind and beliefs that which binds you mentally or physically. You are unlimited! The presence of God is ever with you, inspiring you to rise out of all human concepts of limitation and accept the Truth. You can do whatever you want to do. You can be whatever you want to be. You can have whatever you want to have. But one thing is necessary. You must be able to reach the high consciousness in which you know there are no limitations.

"Life is a mirror and will reflect back to the thinker what he thinks into it." Our thoughts create our reality. So if thoughts are things, think peace, health, wellness, and prosperity. As Ernest Holmes says, "There is a Power for Good in the Universe and you can use it!" May you use it wisely and well.

Week 34
Mad about You

Mad about you. "What exactly does that mean?" you may ask. And here's a tricky thing about the American version of the English language: Sometimes words by themselves have one meaning, and when you put them into a series of words, an idiom, for example, they mean something entirely different. *Mad* by itself means angry, but when you say, "I am mad about you," it means I am head over heels in love with you.

When eating something you really enjoy, another idiom would be, "It's to die for." Now wouldn't it make more sense to say, "It's to live for?" One way, it's your last chance to eat the item in question, and the other way you get to continue eating it.

For our purposes, "mad about you" refers to embodying love within yourself. Ernest Holmes says in *The Science of Mind* textbook, "Man by thinking, can bring into his experience whatsoever he desires—if he thinks correctly, and becomes a living embodiment of his thoughts" (30). How can you have that love affair within that frees you to totally love life? Three things are especially important, and together they are a map, a guide, to a love affair with life. These three things are

1. A positive mental attitude;
2. Authenticity in your life;
3. Purpose in your life.

When your mental attitude is positive, you look at and meet life's challenges calmly and rationally. Praise every situation, even if it is perceived to be bad. See what blessings it holds. Raymond Charles Barker in his book *The Power of Decision* shares this:

> *The atmosphere of praise and thanksgiving is vital in metaphysical practice. It is a mental atmosphere in which ideas are nourished and given their freedom to create their corresponding forms. Your subconscious mind is like a mother's womb. You have implanted it in your decision, which is a seed idea. The subconscious is now at work building a definite identity of thought that will soon emerge in your consciousness. (140)*

You are planting those positive thoughts in Mind, caring for and feeding them with wisdom, and knowing they are so. Even though you may not know exactly how they will come about, when you plant ideas into the Mind of God you can trust the process. Your embodied thoughts will manifest. Release any doubt. Barker continues,

> *Doubt regarding the end result of your demonstration must not enter your thinking. It is to be avoided at all costs. Every time doubt, question or fear begins in your mind, catch yourself and stop it. (140)*

Remember, if you plant cucumbers in the soil, you will get cucumbers. The same thing applies to planting thoughts into minds, so start with a positive and thankful mental attitude. Have an attitude of gratitude and you'll always end up with more to be grateful for.

The second key to that love affair with yourself is to be authentic—be your true self with others. Not every person you meet will be your best friend, but the ones who mean the most to you will always accept you and love you for who you really are.

There is a story about a prince in a land far away and long ago, born with warts all over his face. He was out in public one day when he was just a lad and another boy laughed at him. As a result, he spent most of his youth shut away in his room, and on those occasions when he came out, he would wear a bag over his head. When his father died he became the lord of the kingdom and made an edict that anyone who laughed at him would be beheaded. Being very self-conscious, he still spent much of his time indoors.

One day he heard of a wise man in the mountains who knew the answers to all questions, so he put on his bag and started out. When he got to the wise man he explained his situation and removed the bag. The man smiled at him and the king became furious. He said, "How dare you laugh at me. Don't you know that I am king and can have you beheaded?" The old man assured him that he was merely being pleasant. He asked the king to look more closely at him, and when he did, he noticed an old man with warts all over his face as well. And the king said, "But didn't people laugh at you for having warts?" "Yes," the wise man replied, "but many didn't. I have many friends who see me as I truly am." (www.iloveu love.com/unconditlove/wartking.htm)

Are there things about yourself that you feel are limitations? Could there be a few things that are magnified in your eyes that others could not care less about? Be authentic. Be yourself.

As a student I was involved in public speaking and drama in high school. I especially loved drama because it didn't involve direct eye contact with my audience. Whenever I spoke, I was extremely nervous. In college I took a speech class where all the speeches were videotaped. One particular speech was eye-opening for me. I was speaking about conditioned response. I described Pavlov ringing a bell when he fed his dog and how it soon reached the point where the dog expected food every time he heard the bell ring. I also conveyed the concept of a mother chicken imprinting her baby chicks. When you tap on the ground in front of a baby chick, it will follow you around the room. While giving my speech, I had a baby chick in a brown bag behind me crying, "Cheep, cheep, cheep, cheep." I thought, *Oh my, this speech is awful, I'm not making sense. My heart is racing. This speech is not going well at all.* Then I watched myself on the video and was surprised to see that I did not look the slightest bit nervous. The speech was well paced and I appeared quite confident. That's when it dawned on me that the nervousness was in my eyes only, and that so many of the fears we have aren't even seen by others. Be authentic and others will appreciate you for who you are.

The last key to this love affair with yourself and life is to practice purpose. Many people think purpose needs to be something big and important. But perhaps your purpose is merely to be open to the possibilities of what you can do, how you can help, how you can serve. Do an affirmative prayer treatment that allows you to be open to new ideas. Trust those ideas to come. Sit in meditation after asking this question: What do I need to know? According to Barker,

> *Inspiration can be induced in consciousness. The more you declare that you are inspired, the freer the flow of inspiration. New ideas appear to give you refreshing thought. They prevent mental staleness, which is a dead-end street. They keep a circulation of healthy thinking, which gives the mind a healthy tone.* (143)

Relax into the knowing that inspiration brings ideas that allow us to be on purpose, to love, to help, to serve.

To awaken our love affair with ourselves and our lives we remember to be positive and thankful, to always be ourselves, and to live life on purpose. When you do all that, you'll find it is so easy to be mad about you.

Week 35
A Starbucks Experience

It's always wonderful to have an attitude of gratitude, because in having that outlook, you pave the way for having even more to be grateful for. Being in service to others is also a great way to exercise gratitude. Both of these traits, being grateful and being in service, greatly add to the circulation of life, the idea of giving and receiving.

Starbucks is an excellent example of being in service to others. Why else would a person spend so much for a cup of coffee? I have weaned myself down to one cup of Starbucks at the airport, or when I occasionally meet someone for coffee. This is good for me; I used to be a daily Starbucks visitor, sometimes twice a day. It bugged the heck out of me that what I spent for one cup of coffee would buy a whole can of coffee at the grocery store. How many cups does a can of coffee make? I'm not sure, but

I know that six scoops make a pot of twelve cups, so there are many, many pots that come out of that can.

Why is it so many people go to Starbucks for coffee each day? Part of it is the friendly atmosphere. If you go often enough, they know what you want even before you ask for it. People show up for that friendly atmosphere and perhaps even to affirm their affluence. And Starbucks is never afraid of competition. There can be three or more stores in a single city, some even blocks apart on the same street and each one has its loyal customers.

One of my best friends was not one of them, however. She never set foot in a Starbucks until her granddaughter wanted to stop there after ballet lessons to order the fancy caramel macchiato with 2 percent skim milk, extra hot, and tall (which is really their small). For months they would go through the same routine. But finally it turned out that going to Starbucks with her granddaughter actually gave Grandma the confidence to go in on her own. She had been a little intimidated to order because she wasn't sure she had the right terminology for ordering a fancy cup of coffee, but the barista assured her there was no such thing as an awkward order and said she would help her out—another reason people like going there.

To me, this Starbucks experience is a great analogy for spirituality. People go to church for the friendly atmosphere they find there, and for the inspiration they receive. They could have stayed home, but going makes them feel good. There are certainly many churches to choose from, just as there are many Starbucks. There are also many other coffee shops, and no matter which one you go to, the bottom line is that you *will* receive coffee. Spirituality is no different: no matter what church, mosque, temple, or center you attend, God is there.

Like churches, Starbucks also finds ways to give back to the community and the world. They sell CDs with proceeds going out to various causes and at times a percentage of a day's sales will go to support a local charity. In fact, Starbucks is going to help its workers get a college degree: it's partnering with Arizona State University to make an online undergraduate degree available at a steep discount to any of its 135,000 US employees who work at least 20 hours a week. They are remembering to give thanks. Just as the baristas at Starbucks will help you out when you need it, so will reading metaphysical books, going to classes or doing affirmative prayers. I like to think of Science of Mind as a thinking person's spirituality. When involved in a class, you have the opportunity to share in community with like-minded individuals, ask questions, and get a clear picture of how it applies to your life.

Negative or positive, our thoughts create our reality. Often, synchronistic events will occur before Divine right action presents itself. There is a tale about one woman who did a prayer treatment for a long and healthful life, and then sat in meditation for over an hour. Not too long afterwards she had the inner knowing that God had spoken to her, telling her she would live to be ninety-five. Excited about this, she joined a gym, saw a nutritionist, lost weight, had a face-lift, cut, colored, and styled her hair, and then was hit by a bus and killed. She did get to heaven, and was thrilled there was an afterlife, but she said to God, "Was I hearing things? Did you or did you not say I was going to live to be ninety-five?" "Oh, sorry," he answered. "I didn't recognize you" (dontloseheart.org/?page_id=1936).

You can change yourself in ways that are important to you, knowing they will make you feel better, and still remain your authentic self—already perfect, whole, and complete.

Week 36
Move from Headlines to Heartlines

What happens when we truly comprehend that we can live our lives authentically? It is such a freeing feeling. When we are living our truth we soon find ourselves around other people living their truth, and that's real freedom.

"Move From Headlines to Heartlines" is a title from a deck of *The Life Lift-off Cards* created by Michael Beckwith. The card reads,

> *The daily headlines describe a global culture that has been cut off from its Soul. The good news is that there is an emergent culture rising up and announcing that these headlines are not reality. Heartlines are being activated around the globe, building a spiritual infrastructure that reveals the triumph of peace, compassion, honor, and dignity for all. Are you aligning your consciousness with these heartlines?*

Move from headlines to heartlines. It does seem to be true that negativity gets the spotlight in the news. As already mentioned, Ernest Holmes got up every morning, read the newspaper, and then set it aside saying, "There isn't a word of truth in there." Because he didn't buy into the doom-and-gloom race consciousness presented there, he allowed himself freedom from worry and negativity.

From headlines to heartlines. Head refers to logic and how ideas are viewed from a more practical outlook, and heart deals with the emotional aspect of a situation. When we can blend the two together, we get the best results. The heart in your prayer needs to be evident: a Divine knowing that it will absolutely come into being. Then the Law, the practical, logical process, brings it about.

Can we view life situations through our heartline? We certainly can. Loving parents do this all the time. We do it for our friends, and they return the favor. Too often when something major happens, especially a difficult challenge, the headlines are the initial fearful reaction to the situation and the heartlines denote the calmer response.

A couple very dear to me have a son whose girlfriend had a baby while they were still in high school. The headlines came when my friend and his wife first found out. *What would people think of them? After all, they raised their children to be more responsible than this.* The heartlines came as they planned for their granddaughter's birth. Their son learned that his parent's love is truly unconditional.

A friend or family member tells you about the death of a loved one. The headlines are that this person died. The heartlines are the compassion we share in helping them go through those first few weeks or months. Sometimes, and probably most often, those heartlines are expressed by just being available to listen or to put an arm around someone while sitting in silence.

Contrary to what some may believe, heartlines are not about being against war. They are about being for peace. Consider any situation in your life—what are you for? I am for kindness, peace, truth, love, and all positive God qualities. I am for wholeness and happiness, and true joy. I am for accentuating the positive. In his cards Michael Beckwith states,

> *Heartlines are being activated around the globe, building a spiritual infrastructure that reveals the triumph of peace, compassion, honor and dignity for all. Are you aligning your consciousness with these heartlines?*

The more that people live in peace, love, harmony, truth, and kindness, the more they inspire others to follow their example, and the closer we are to peace on earth. Don Miguel Ruiz, in the final chapter of *The Fifth Agreement* enlightens,

> *I invite you to participate in a dream for humanity, one in which all of us can live in harmony, truth and love.*
>
> *In this dream, people of all religions and all philosophies are not just welcome, but respected. Each of us has the right to believe whatever we want to believe, to follow any religion or philosophy we want to follow. It doesn't matter whether we believe in Christ, Allah, Brahma, Buddha or any other master; everybody is welcome to share this dream . . . . If you can feel the truth behind these words, then let's make one more agreement: Help me change the world.*
>
> *Of course, the very first question is How can I change the world? The answer is easy. By changing your world. When I ask you to help me to change the world, I'm not talking about planet earth. I'm referring to the virtual world that exists in your head.*

The change begins with you. You will not help me to change the world if you don't change your own world first.

You will change the world by loving yourself, by enjoying life, by making your personal world a dream of heaven. And I ask you for your help because you are the only one who can change your world. If you decide that you want to change your world, the easiest way is by using the tools that are nothing but common sense. The Five Agreements are tools to change the world. If you are impeccable with your word, if you don't take anything personally, if you don't make assumptions, if you always do your best, and if you are skeptical while listening, there will be peace. (221-222)

Once again here is someone reminding us that having a good life is an inside job. Just imagine if everyone in the world decided to really enjoy themselves, to completely love themselves just as they are, to practice peace and harmony. That would be heaven on earth.

It's interesting how Don Miguel Ruiz dreamed of each of us having the freedom to choose what faith, if any, we follow. This also allows for us to not believe in God.

An atheist was taking a walk through the woods, admiring all that the "accident of evolution" had created. "What majestic trees! What a powerful river! What beautiful animals!" he said to himself. As he walked alongside the river he heard a rustling in the bushes behind him. He turned to look and saw a seven-foot grizzly charging toward him. He ran as fast as he could up the path. He looked over his shoulder and saw that the bear was closing in on him. He ran even faster, so scared that tears were coming to his eyes. He looked over his shoulder again and the bear was even closer. His heart was pumping frantically and he tried to run faster still. He tripped and fell to the ground. He rolled over to pick himself up, but saw the bear . . . right on top of him . . . reaching for him with the left paw and raising his right paw to strike him.

At that instant the atheist cried out, "Oh, my God, please help me..." Suddenly, time stopped. The bear froze in motion. The forest was ever so silent. Even the river ceased to flow. A brilliant ray of light emerged from the sky and shone upon the man. A powerful voice spoke to him: "You have denied my existence for all of these years; you teach others that I do not exist and you credit creation to a cosmic accident. Do you expect me to help you out of this predicament? Am I to count you now as a believer?"

The atheist blinked directly into the light and replied, "It would be hypocritical of me to convert to Christianity after all these years, but could you instead make the bear a Christian?"

"Very well," said the voice from above. The bright light disappeared. All of a sudden, life resumed around the man. The river ran again. The forest became alive once more with the gentle sounds of nature. The bear stirred. Slowly, he lowered his right paw, brought both paws together, bowed his head and graciously spoke: "Lord, for this food which I am about to receive, I am truly thankful."
(naute.com/jokes/atheist.phtml)

Everyone has the right to believe as they please, and some do not believe in God, but when I look around at nature and the beauty that surrounds me, it is too magnificent to have happened by accident. I believe in One Creative Power and know there are many pathways to that Power.

In *Wisdom of the Ages*, Wayne Dyer has a chapter titled, "Reverence for Nature." In it he speaks of the wisdom of Native Americans whose words reflect reverence for all that is sacred in our natural world. He speaks of Chief Seattle and his speech to Congress about "the web of life," the understanding that our actions affect others and how we should act in a way that does not harm Mother Nature. He writes of Oren Lyons, an Onondaga Faithkeeper who tells of his people making decisions based on preserving our natural resources so the next seven generations to come will see the beauty and majesty of this planet. He speaks of Wolf Song of the Benaki Tribe who says,

> *To honor and respect means to think of the land and the water and plants and animals that live here as having a right equal to our own to be here. We are not the supreme and all-knowing beings, living at the top of the pinnacle of evolution, but in fact we are members of the sacred hoop of life, along with the trees and rocks, the coyotes and the eagles and fish and toad; each fulfills its purpose. They each perform their given task in the sacred hoop, and we have one, too.* (116-117)

It seems we are forgetting in all of our technological advances to be friendly to our own environment. There is a fine line in the phrase, free to be me. We must be informed human beings as we make our life choices.

The very basis of a democratic society requires that we give up some of our freedom to be protected by the very same society we are living in. So, "free to be me" is the same as saying, "I am free to express myself authentically." When I am living my truth, and I can be around other people who are living their truth, that's freedom. When collectively we decide to move from headlines to heartlines, instead of complaining about what's happening in the world around us, we will see what we each can do to make a difference. Maybe that means buying a hybrid car or solar panels for our home, or maybe it means doing an affirmative prayer now and again about the significance of the web of life. Everything we do and say affects the world around us, so make your words and actions be ones that help build a happy, prosperous, healthy way of life.

Week 37
Moving with the Current

When challenges present themselves, take a deep breath and know that God surrounds and supports you always. Life becomes for us what we think it to be, so think calm, peace, joy, health, and prosperity.

When we contemplate moving with the current, we are reminded that life doesn't have to be hard. Remembering the law of least resistance, Raymond Holliwell reminds us in *Working with the Law* that we win an argument by refusing to argue. Being an ocean-loving California girl for the major part of my life, I can remember being told to swim with the current, parallel to shore, to avoid being caught in the riptide. A rip current, the proper term for riptide, is a current of water that can knock you off your feet and carry you a good distance out to sea. It does not drag you underwater. It is formed by breaking waves where the water returning back out to sea from either side of the current converges, and often you can see it. Water from both sides of the rip current rushes back out from one place. To escape, you don't swim against a rip current but instead swim parallel to the shore until you are out of the current's pull, and then swim back to shore. That is the path of least resistance.

Rowing a boat or canoe is always much easier when you are paddling downstream. Flying a small plane is easier and quicker when catching a tailwind. In life, as well, going with the flow is a great lesson. Now, going with the flow doesn't mean giving up your personal power and acquiescing to everyone else's plans and wishes, but it does mean being agreeable with life. Planning for upcoming events is great, but being open and receptive to new ideas and changes along the way can make events even better.

Being in the classroom for more than twenty-five years tuned me in to "teaching moments." When something like the JFK assassination or the Challenger explosion happens—this is not the time to turn the television off and work on a grammar assignment. In the movie *Freedom Writers*, there is a perfect example of a teaching moment. While a young teacher is working with some pretty tough students, unbeknownst to her a picture is being passed around the room. It is a Latino student's stereotyped drawing of his black classmate with exaggerated big lips. When she finally notices it, the teacher jumps in proactively, talking about prejudice and Holocaust victims and an artist who drew pictures of Jewish people in caricature. This leads to a discussion of Nazi Germany and a unit on what one country did to others.

When going with the flow, moving constructively with the current, negative energy is diffused. Think of yourself as a river flowing downstream. What is it that might obstruct you, what could impede your path? Is it another person, a job, resentment, the inability to forgive and move on? Whatever it is, could it be easier to let the situation go, to stop feeding it negative energy?

If you are still agonizing or angry at another person's action or words from the past, chances are that person isn't even aware of your feelings, while it may be eating you alive. If you are the only person suffering from the resentment, why hang on to it?

We can all learn a lesson from nature and the animals that reside there. The beaver never thinks, "Oh, Mom loved my brother more than me," or "I know that guy planned to cut down the exact tree I had my eyes on." No, beavers go with the flow; they ride the current as it comes.

Sometimes it takes several similar experiences before we take the blinders off our eyes and wake up to our own magnificence. Each person is born into this Universe to experience the goodness of God; some people just don't recognize that goodness is their birthright. It is not always easy to acknowledge that we are responsible for our own lives. It's so much easier to blame someone else, to become a victim. Ernest Holmes tells us this in *The Science of Mind* textbook:

> *Life is a blessing or a curse, according to the use we make of it. In the long run, no one judges us but ourselves. We believe in a law that governs all things and all people. If we make mistakes, we suffer. We are our own reward and our own punishment.* (383)

So as things happen, we can move with the current. Not all of our decisions are the best ones. When they are not, we can make a new decision. Some people are afraid of failing so they resist trying anything new. *Chicken Soup for the Soul* shares with us a message originally printed in the *Wall Street Journal* by the United Technologies Corporation.

> *You've failed many times, although you may not remember.*
>
> *You fell down the first time you tried to walk. You almost drowned the first time you tried to swim, didn't you?*

Did you hit the ball the first time you swung a bat?
Heavy hitters, the ones who hit the most home
runs, also strike out a lot.
R.H. Macy failed seven times before his store in
New York caught on.
English novelist John Creasey got 753 rejection
slips before he published 564 books.
Babe Ruth struck out 1,330 times, but he also hit
714 home runs.
Don't worry about failure.
Worry about the chances you miss when you don't
even try. (235)

Moving with the current means being in action. If something's not working, do an affirmative prayer treatment; treat and move your feet. If you are lonely or bored and you sit at home and watch TV, is your life going to change for the better? No. Moving with the current means not being stagnant but trying new things, connecting with life and with other people. Eric Butterworth, author of *Spiritual Economics*, says,

> *The glorious truth is that you are a very special person, and you always have something special working within you. The whole Universe is on your side. Life is forever biased on the side of healing, on the side of overcoming, on the side of success. When you get yourself centered in the universal flow, you become synchronized with this Divine bias for good. Amazing things can and will unfold. Some will call them miracles, but you will accept them as the perfectly natural function of the Divine process.* (24)

With each breath of life may we become more and more aware that we are part of the current, part of the Divine flow of the goodness of life. Release and let go, and let God.

Week 38
Love, Laugh, and Be Well

Since love is actually a synonym for God, it is easy to see the wisdom in loving and being well. When you choose this state of being, laughter is naturally more abundant. Ernest Holmes explains:

> *Love is the self-givingness of Spirit through the desire of Life to express Itself in terms of Creation. Emerson says that Love is a synonym for God. We are also told in the New Testament that "he that loveth not, knoweth not God; for God is Love. Love is free from condemnation, even as it is free from fear. Love is a cosmic force whose sweep is irresistible." Science of Mind (608)*

God's wisdom lights our way and, when we partner with that Mind, the Mind of God, life just seems to run more smoothly.

Love, laugh, and be well speaks to the idea of seeing the good in each and every situation. When we can find the good, shift happens. But let's expand that idea of positive goodness. Let's expand it to something that is often expressed when we are feeling joy, laughter, or love. Holisticonline.com tells us this:

> *Patients, doctors and health-care professionals are all finding that laughter may indeed be the best medicine. Laughing is found to lower blood pressure, reduce stress hormones, increase muscle flexion, and boost immune function by raising levels of infection-fighting T-cells, disease-fighting proteins called Gamma-interferon and B-cells, which produce disease-destroying antibodies. Laughter also triggers the release of endorphins, the body's natural pain-killers, and produces a general sense of wellbeing.*

> *Laughter is infectious. Hospitals around the country are incorporating formal and informal laughter therapy programs into their therapeutic regimens. In countries such as India, laughing clubs—in which participants gather in the early morning for the sole purpose of laughing—are becoming as popular as Rotary Clubs in the United States. Humor is a universal language. It's a contagious emotion and a natural diversion. It brings other people in and breaks down barriers. Best of all it is free and has no known side reactions.*

Have you ever been down in the dumps, really sad, maybe crying, when a friend or teacher helped you see a lighter side to even the worst situation? Getting your mind off feelings of negativity always improves a situation. Fond memories will sometimes help; so might singing old songs that once made you feel good. Pat Campbell in her book, *Giving God A Good Time*, remembers listening to the Eagles. They combined rock, folk, and country, and they always had such great harmonies. About five years ago they came out with a new album, *Long Road Out of Eden*. This was after a twenty-year tiff that had broken the band apart. At that time they swore they would never play together again, and yet time healed the wounds and they reunited to discover they still had that wonderful harmony (135).

Change your focus and soon you will be able to laugh and be well. We are always at choice and we can resolve at any time to release our discord and come into harmony. One person who chose to do this on a large scale was Dr. Martin Luther King Jr. He grew up in a society of discord and disharmony, a country where discrimination was a common, everyday occurrence. Yet, Dr. King was a deeply spiritual man and knew this disharmony was not God-ordained, so he took great strides to change the world in non-violent ways. He said,

> *Hatred paralyzes life; love releases it. Hatred confuses life; love harmonizes it. Hatred darkens life; love illuminates it.* (goodreads.com)

How do we create a life of harmony, laughter, and love? It's an inside job. It starts on the inside of each one of us and spirals out. We must express it in our individual lives, and then we will send it out.

How often has an incident made you feel that it was randomly the most unfortunate situation that could ever have transpired, only to find in the next few days it was actually a blessing? Sometimes unexpected events lead to wonderful new ideas. When you look at the history of great scientists, you notice that many of their inventions were owing to mistakes. Of course, much hard work and research helped as well, but some people were simply lucky! Or maybe they were actually blessed. Consider the invention of Saccharin:

> *As we all know, Saccharin is an artificial sweetener that is commonly used in our daily lives to prepare*

various dishes. The basic substance in Saccharin is benzoic sulfinide, which has no food energy and is much sweeter than the sucrose commonly found in fruits and vegetables.

Saccharin was first discovered by a chemist named Constantin Fahlberg when he didn't wash his hands after spending his day at the office. It was 1879 when Fahlberg was trying to discover the new uses of coal tar. After working all day at the office, Fahlberg went home and found something very strange. He noticed that the roll he was eating started tasting sweet. On asking his wife, he found that the rolls were made in the usual manner and that his wife didn't find the rolls sweet. That's when Fahlberg realized that the taste was coming from his hands, which he had not washed. The next day, Fahlberg took a sample to his lab, where he dis- covered Saccharin. (Wikipedia)

Some people might call this a random accident, but perhaps it was Divine right action taking place.

To love, laugh, and be well can translate simply to mean seeing the lighter side of any situation. Deepak Chopra, in *The Seven Spiritual Laws of Success,* calls this the law of least resistance. He shares this:

If you observe nature at work, you will see that the least effort is expended. Grass doesn't try to grow; it just grows. Fish don't try to swim; they just swim. Birds don't try to fly; they just fly. The earth doesn't try to spin on its own axis; it is the nature of the earth to spin with dizzying speed and to hurtle through space. It is the nature of babies to be in bliss. It is the nature of the stars to glitter and sparkle. And it is human nature to make our dreams manifest into physical form, easily and effortlessly. (53-54)

Sometimes we spend too much time worrying about whether we can do something instead of just doing it. Occasionally, someone comes to us, blustering loudly about the awful mess he or she is in. We can feed that frenzy, or we can be the calm in the face of the storm and merely by our quiet, calm response can de-energize volatile situations. Any time a person comes to you with a problem and you successfully turn it around into an amusing moment, you help them to laugh and be well.

I spoke earlier of love being a synonym for God. When you listen to people and allow them to sort out their own ideas, you are expressing as God's love. Deepak continues in the chapter "The Law of Least Effort," linking the idea of love and prosperity together:

> *Least effort is expended when your actions are motivated by love, because nature is held together by the energy of love. When you seek power and control over other people, you waste energy. When you seek money or power for the sake of ego, you spend energy chasing the illusion of happiness instead of enjoying happiness in the moment. When you seek money for personal gain only, you cut off the flow of energy to yourself and interfere with the expression of nature's intelligence. But when your actions are motivated by love, your energy multiplies and accumulates—and the surplus energy you gather and enjoy can be channeled to create anything that you want, including unlimited wealth.* (55)

Do you remember all you learned about money when you were young? Phrases like, "Money is the root of all evil" and "Money doesn't grow on trees" were common. Well, money actually does come from trees, but you get my point. What else do you remember hearing?

Having money is not a bad thing, but when you have it, it is best to continue to circulate it. Like Dolly Levi says in

The Matchmaker by Thornton Wilder, "Money is like manure, it is meant to be spread around, encouraging young things to grow." It is the hoarding of money that is actually where trouble comes into play. Money alone cannot buy happiness, but add love, joy, and beauty and share with others and you can experience the true value of happiness.

Deepak Chopra says there are three components to the law of least resistance: acceptance, responsibility, and defenselessness.

Acceptance simply means that you make a commitment: "Today I will accept people, situations, circumstances, and events as they occur. This moment is as it should be" (63). An accident happens; someone hits your car in a roundabout. You realize this happened because someone was not focused, or perhaps they didn't know much about driving in roundabouts. You say to yourself, "I'm not going to get angry about it because my getting angry at this other driver's mistake will not erase the fact that it happened. I will make sure everyone is okay and exchange insurance information." Or, you may find you do not like your child's girlfriend or boyfriend, but decide that you will be accepting of his or her choice of friends.

Responsibility means not blaming anyone or anything for your situation, including yourself (63-64). Do you ever notice that you are the easiest person to blame for things? *I'm not sticking to my diet—I could have handled that situation better—why does it seem as though I'm always late?* Again, you are in the traffic roundabout and you hit the driver in front of you because she stopped suddenly for someone else. Accept responsibility. Exchange insurance information, be happy you had the foresight to have insurance and do not torture yourself about the accident. Accept that it happened. In the past you might have agonized over the accident well into the night or even into the next week or two. Accidents happen. No one sits at home planning one: "Hmmm, I think I'll have an accident tomorrow, the roundabout by the high school would be a great spot." Take responsibility and vow to be more focused the next time you are in the roundabout.

Deepak declares defenselessness as the third component of the law of least effort:

> Which means that your awareness is established in defenselessness, and you have relinquished your need to convince others of your point of view. If you observe people around you, you'll see they spend ninety-nine percent of their time defending their points of view. If you just relinquish the need to defend your point of view, you will, in that relinquishment, gain access to enormous amounts of energy that have been previously wasted (60).

Raymond Holliwell calls this, "Winning an argument by refusing to argue" (135). Not accepting the bait of someone tempting you to go ballistic allows you to maintain a laugh-and-be-well state of mind, though you may need to remove yourself from the presence of the instigator, and perhaps be in the company of another positive like-minded individual.

God's wisdom lights our way, and, when we partner with that Mind, the Mind of God, life just seems to run more smoothly. Love, laugh, and be well while finding the good in each and every situation and you will see shift happen almost effortlessly.

Week 39
My God Is an Awesome God

My God is an awesome God. If it's true, and I believe it is, that we are all one, then your God, my God, our collective God is an awesome God as well.

In my younger years I would sing, "My God is an awesome God, He reigns forever and ever." That power, that God essence, that Divine Intelligence has been creating life out of itself for eons. What has transpired on Earth during this span is rather amazing, pretty awesome.

As human beings, we too are quite amazing. The world around us is remarkable, and we are likewise extraordinary. When you think of all the idiosyncrasies of all the species of plants and animals on this planet, it is all too incredible to have happened by accident. How can a bumblebee fly? That is an act of seeming impossibility, that little body and those fragile little wings. What makes a firefly light up, or a homing pigeon know how to come home?

My husband, Gary, and I love ocean cruises. He has taken at least four times as many as I have, but we both agree that when you are standing at the back of the boat in the middle of the ocean, with the vastness of God's majesty spread out around you, it is stunning to stop and consider all that God has created.

And isn't it amazing what we as human beings, with the use of that Divine Mind of God, have created? Each of us daily creates our own lives. Do we make mistakes? At times, but we usually make the best possible choices in the moment. For many of us, that applies also to our parents. We may not have agreed with some of the decisions our parents made, but they were most often made to the best of their knowledge at the time.

In the movie, *Conversations with God*, we learn a little about the life of Neale Donald Walsh prior to the writing of his book, *Conversations with God*. At a later point in the movie, after many sales proved his book popular, an incident happened at a book signing at a Barnes and Noble. A woman confronted Walsh, saying, "You believe your God is a loving God? My husband and I raised a baby from birth, never telling him he was adopted until he was fourteen and we thought he could understand the situation. He became sullen and wouldn't speak to us. We finally promised him that when he was eighteen we would try to find his birth mother." Walsh asked her if that worked out, and she said, as she sobbed, "He's dead. He died looking for her." He was quiet a moment, and then went within. In a few moments he looked at her and said, "I don't know how I know this, but I do. He is with her now; dying was the only way he could find her. She has been dead for some time." The woman calmed down and people in the audience came to console her and speak to her. The scene ended as he was leaving, saying to his assistant, "I don't know how I knew that, but I did."

The point is, all we can do—ever—is the best we can do. Our parents did just that, the best they could do under the circumstances they were in. My older brother used to complain about how he was being treated by our father. His youth leader overheard him and gave him some of the best advice anyone could be given: "If you don't like the way you are treated, make a point to do things differently when you are given the chance. By doing so, you are being proactive." Ernest Holmes says,

> *Thought is the conscious activity of the one thinking, and works as he directs, through Law; and this Law may be consciously set in motion. This law will work for him to the fullest extent of his belief and understanding of it. A realization of the Presence of God is the most powerful healing agency known to man. (Science of Mind, 145)*

As already mentioned, when students pass all the Science of Mind classes after two years, they are eligible for the 300 curriculum to train to become licensed practitioners and do prayer treatments for others. They learn how to remember and hold the truth for all who come to them for service, the truth being that they are each perfect, whole, and complete just as they are. The practitioner is prompting them to remember who they truly are, and to heal the consciousness of each individual.

At times, problems that interfere with a healthy consciousness stem from fear—from not liking a job or a relationship, for instance, but being afraid of what would happen without the familiar. It is my belief that risk taking is what alleviates fear. Have you heard the saying, "Face the fear and it will disappear"?

In his book *Wisdom of the Ages*, Wayne Dyer says to take the risk, go on with life as if failure were not a consideration. He says, "It is better to jump in and experience life, than to stand on the sidelines fearing that something might go wrong." If you are unhappy with some aspect of your life, if you really hate it, what is that negative emotion doing to your body? Dyer says, "It is far better to have acted and produced results that you will grow from than to ignore your nature and live in fear" (154).

What if you spent your life fearing without ever learning to really live? George Bernard Shaw, one of my favorite Irish playwrights, put it so well:

> *This is the true joy of life: The being used for a purpose recognized by yourself as a mighty one. The being a force of nature, instead of a feverish, selfish little clod of ailments and grievances complaining that the world will not devote itself to making you happy. I am of the opinion that my life belongs to the whole community, and as long as I live, it is my privilege to do for it whatever I can.*
>
> *I want to be thoroughly used up when I die—for the harder I work, the more I live. I rejoice in life for its own sake. Life is no "brief candle" to me; it is a sort of splendid torch which I have got hold of for the moment, and I want to make it burn as brightly as possible before handing it on to future generations.* (oblations.blogspot.com/2007/10/ george-bernard-shaw-true-joy-in-life.html)

God is right here where we are; life is right here where we are. Each of us is the star in the movie of our own life. Each of us makes our own life happen, and it is an awesome life. Our lives mirror God and, gosh darn it, if our God is an awesome God, then it follows that we are awesome too.

Week 40
Picture Frame Memories

When I think of picture frame memories I think of the Barbara Streisand, Robert Redford movie, *The Way We Were*. Barbara plays an intelligent girl who was always the awkward teenager but grew into an attractive woman. Because she was unappealing in her youth, she carries with her that nagging feeling that she is never enough.

Sometimes I fall into that trap. In my youth I thought of myself as heavier than I should be, but when I look at pictures of myself from back then I long to be the same size. Perhaps some of you can relate to this memory.

Memories can be fond or painful. When some event stands out in our minds, and it is absolutely the most vivid image, I think of that as being a picture frame memory. Where were you when you heard that Martin Luther King Jr., JFK, or Robert Kennedy was shot? Where were you when the space shuttle exploded, or the Twin Towers were attacked? What song was playing on the radio when you met your first love? Which birthday in your past was the most memorable?

Events stand out in our memories because they mark either high or low points in our lives. While they are from our past, they teach us very vital present-day lessons that come with some bad news and some good news. The bad news is that in our lives there are memorable, average, and unpleasant times. The good news is that there are memorable, average, and pleasant times. Whatever happens in your life, you have the ability to choose how you react.

Dennis Merritt Jones in *The Art of Being* was speaking to a teller in a bank who had a thirty-year-old son living with her. She constantly shared that she was feeling frustrated with him. One day she said, "I can't wait until next year." When he asked her why, she replied, "Because next year can't possibly be as bad as this year." "Oh, really?" he said. "What will you be doing differently that will change the situation?" She said she didn't follow him so he explained. "It sounds to me as though you have two choices to change the situation with your son. One is to very firmly and lovingly tell him you expect him to be out of your house by a certain date. The other is to change your mind about resenting his being there." When she understood this, she had the chance to get out of her inactivity about the situation (23-24). As Einstein once so wisely explained, insanity is doing things exactly the same way you have been doing them and expecting them to change.

It's actually good we go through highs and lows in life because it proves we are alive and growing with experience. Go into a hospital room and watch the lines on the monitor going up and down and the "bleep, bleep" that accompanies them. The highs and lows on the screen and the auditory bleeps from the monitor indicate what? They indicate life.

So much of what we've been through has given us strength to carry on and the wisdom to be compassionate with others going through similar situations. Those times have provided necessary evolutionary changes in our lives. And the lows give us a way to recognize the highs.

Some of our standout memories really do need to remain in the back of our minds; in fact, even some of the painful memories colored with understanding can be stored. The memories we need to release are those of resentment. When we rehash what he or she said or did, it's like as the Buddha says, "taking poison and never finding the antidote" (goodreads.com/...?603179). The person who said it or did it may not even know you are bothered. Angry, resentful feelings can cause health issues, but when those feelings are released and no longer eating away at you, you may find you no longer have a pain in the neck or a pain in the back.

Louise Hay has an excellent book called *You Can Heal Yourself*, which encourages people to recognize the "dis-ease" in their lives that may be causing their conditions. When we understand that we are in control of our lives, and that ideas rule the world, we can concentrate on keeping them positive. Raymond Charles Barker in *The Power of Decision*, declares

> *When ideas are positive and are given freedom to unfold in a mind that loves what it is doing, then they do rule the world of such an individual. Such directed thinking cannot be defeated by person, place or situation. It always is victorious and successful.* (156)

So, if you are lonely, worried, or feeling bored, it is up to you to do something about it. Call a friend, write in your journal, ask someone to do a prayer treatment for you, or just get outside and walk. So many things in nature are the very things that remind us of what life is all about—the new daffodils or crocuses poking their heads through the soil, beautiful sunsets, birds playing in the bushes and trees. It is important to remember that we are always at choice.

Barker reminds us that "the person who cannot stop worrying is the person who wants to worry" (155). And that is true about any negative emotion. You might say, "I'm lonely, nobody is talking to me," and yet you don't step forward yourself to say something to somebody.

When I moved into my first house in Washington, Gary and I were carrying boxes up the stairs as the woman on the floor below us was looking out the window. I waved, and she pulled back into the room away from the window. I immediately thought, *Oh, she's having a hard time with my being white and Gary being black.*

A few days later I was baking cookies for church. Our new home was a house that had been divided into four units and since all the units were connected, I figured the other tenants could smell the cookies so I made a few extra for them. When I knocked on the door of the neighbor who had been staring out the window, she invited me in for a cup of tea. That's when I discovered she was actually very shy, which was the reason she initially backed away from the window.

As Don Miguel Ruiz in *The Four Agreements* reminds us, "Don't make assumptions." Always be the one who takes a chance that the world is good. Always believe in yourself. Raymond Charles Barker remarks,

> *The you that the Infinite created has been waiting for your recognition of yourself as it. It is like a baby chicken in the eggshell waiting for the first crack in the shell to find its real existence. Correct self-curiosity causes the shell to find its real existence. Correct self-curiosity causes the shell of your fixed human opinions to crack so that the real self can appear in your consciousness and grasp creative ideas.* (158-159)

The low moments in life supply the opportunities to realize there is something better on the other side of the shell. But what about illness? Sickness appears to the rational mind to be out of our control. Ernest Holmes clarifies this in *The Science of Mind:*

> *Health and sickness are largely externalizations*
> *of our dominant mental and spiritual states.*
> *An emotional shock, or a mind filled with thoughts*
> *of fear, has been known to cause the momentary*
> *stoppage of the heart. Physicians now testify that,*
> *under stress, particularly anger, the blood leaves*
> *a chemical deposit around the joints in the body.*
> *Worry, fear, anger, jealousy, and other emotional*
> *conditions are mental in nature, and as such are*
> *being recognized as the hidden cause of a large*
> *part of all the physical suffering to which the flesh*
> *is heir. A normal healthy mind reflects itself in a*
> *healthy body, and conversely, an abnormal mental*
> *state expresses its corresponding condition in some*
> *physical condition. Thoughts are things!* (144)

Because thoughts are things, they may sometimes become broken. They show up as lack, depression, ill health, or problems with finances. They show up quite often because we have forgotten the truth about ourselves. The truth, I remind you again, is that we are each of us perfect, whole, and complete, just as we are. When you are in a low spot, a way out is to ask a Science of Mind practitioner to do a prayer treatment for you. A practitioner knows the truth for you until you can remember it for yourself. You can learn more about this philosophy and the truth of who you are through classes at a Center for Spiritual Living near you. Does that mean we should not go to doctors when we are ill or hurt? No. It means we accept all the help that is available. Holmes says, "Anything that helps to overcome suffering is good, whether it be a pill or a prayer" (*Science of Mind*, 191.)

Picture frame memories allow our recollections to rise to the surface of our minds. Temper or release the emotional attachment to the painful memories and enjoy those that are loving and wonderful. As the highs and lows in life remind us that we are alive, we do well to also remember that we have so much life left to live. Now is the time to be the bleeps on the monitor of life and save that flat line for much, much later.

Week 41
Ride the Tides of March

Have you ever wondered about the Ides of March, otherwise known as the fifteenth of March? In Shakespeare's *Julius Caesar*, the soothsayer warns, "Beware the Ides of March." Since Caesar was actually killed on that day, he probably should have heeded that advice. A very delightful short play entitled, *Great Caesar's Ghost* by Lewy Olfson is about an absent-minded soothsayer who knows he must warn Caesar but has a hard time remembering what the warning is. He can't recall if it's the brides of March, or the prides, or the tides, or some other caution.

This same type of confusion can find itself at home in our lives when we lose focus, when we lose our sense of balance. Not surprisingly, in the insect world there are insects that innately know the necessity of precise balance. The trap-door spider builds its nest using a pile of sand at its front door. The sand is built up using the angle of repose theory to an exact balance so that when the prey steps on it, it disturbs the balance and the ant or other unsuspecting victim comes sliding down into the spider's nest.

Do you ever feel you are sliding downward, perhaps by continuing a relationship that's not working, a job that's sapping your joy and energy, an endless pile of bills, or health issues you wish you could release? Do you spend too much energy worrying? How much energy do you spend on the good that's happening in your life?

When I realize I'm feeling bogged down by life, I actually sit down and list my blessings so I can visually see and concentrate on them. In most cases, the positives on my list far outweigh anything that bothers me.

Letting go of what no longer serves you can take incredible courage. A friend of mine was married for over thirty years to a man who was an alcoholic. The last ten years they were together he was agoraphobic; he would never leave his home. For the first eight years of his agoraphobia, she stayed home with him, making excuses to friends and family. Finally she decided to leave home to go to church, and then to a class, and then to church activities. After two more years she gave her husband the ultimatum get help or she was leaving. He never got help. She has found she is incredibly happy on her own and says she will always love her ex-husband but now realizes he must make his own decision to be well.

When we are in a situation we don't like, we can stay there and be miserable, or we can choose to make changes in our lives. That is why the title of this essay, "Ride the Tides of March," seems so relevant to me—because Life is worth the ride. We can ride *through* anything. It's when we are stuck and do nothing about it that we are slowly eaten up on the inside.

Have you ever had an acquaintance tell you the same drama over and over? One day the actual drama did end, but the story went on forever and ever, taking on a life of its own, day after day, month after month, year after year. Eventually that story became their very identity. We don't have to live this way. We can choose to focus on the possibilities, and ride the tides. Ernest Holmes says in *The Science of Mind*, "In dealing with Mind, we are dealing with a Force we cannot fool" (153). If we are focused on negative thoughts from the past, we have no room for the real magic of the present moment, and what lies beyond. Dr. Holmes goes on to say,

> *Do we desire to live in a world peopled with friends who love us, surrounded by things beautiful and pleasing? There is but one way, and this is as certain as the sun that shines. DAILY WE MUST CONTROL ALL THOUGHT THAT DENIES THE REAL; AFFIRM THE DIVINE PRESENCE WITHIN US; then, as the mist disappears before the sun, so shall adversity melt before the shining radiance of our exalted thought!* (147)

Something else we can learn to do while riding the tides is to let go of the need to be right. A previous minister of mine once said, "I'd rather be healed than be right."

It's a little known fact that Julius Caesar did not die from stab wounds by Brutus, but rather, was poisoned. During a sumptuous banquet which they both attended on that fateful Ides of March, Brutus slipped some poisonous hemlock leaves into Julius' salad, thus making the world's first Caesar salad (and no, that's not the joke...wait for it...). When Julius slumped over into his salad, Brutus feigned concern and asked, "My dear friend Julius, how many hemlock leaves have you eaten?" To which Julius gasped in reply, "Ate two, Brute." (joke-of-the-day.com/jokes/beware-ides-march")

Remember to stay focused, enjoy what's happening in your present day life, and learn to recognize when it is important to be right. Let yourself ride the tides of happiness, love, and positive thoughts.

Week 42
Real Magic

As wonderful as mothers are, you'd think the tradition of celebrating Mother's Day would date back to ancient times, and yet the tradition in the United States, according to Wikipedia, didn't start until over a century ago in 1908 in Grafton, West Virginia. It began when a grown daughter, Miss Anna Jarvis, decided that too often grown children became so preoccupied with their own families that they often neglected their own mothers. She and her mother were very close and when she went off to college the separation was distressing for her, but she believed in education so she stuck it out. She came home qualified to teach public education.

A year later, in 1905, her mother died, and she was a little gloomy thinking of all the things she could have done or should have done. On the second Sunday in May she invited a houseful of friends over to tell them about her new campaign. She announced her idea to establish a day to honor mothers nationwide—Mother's Day—which met with unanimous support.

She wrote to Andrews Methodist Church in Grafton, West Virginia, where her mother had taught Sunday School for twenty years. They agreed to hold the first celebration and at the end of the service they gave each mother in the congregation a carnation, Anna's mother's favorite flower. On May 8, 1914, President Woodrow Wilson signed a proclamation designating the second Sunday in May, Mother's Day. (Wikpedia)

Very often it is in families that dreams begin to be built, sometimes from the nurturing that occurs there, or the lack of nurturing that gives us the resolve to do something different. The real life magic comes when we realize we have the ability to shape our existence, with the partnership of God. We are cause to our own effect in life, but when we go within and recognize our connection to God, we allow that inspiration to spiral us forward.

When we realize God is within us, just as we are in God, that's when real magic occurs. God is everywhere present. It is up to us to find our own connection. Just as electricity was always present before man discovered it and learned how to channel its use, everyone has the ability to connect with God. When we recognize that ability, it is real magic.

We are continually learning and expanding our consciousness as life brings us new experiences. If something happens that isn't to our liking, we have the ability to look at that situation in a different way or take steps to change the situation. We always have choice.

Dr. Holmes tells us that the only heaven and hell are the ones we create for ourselves here on earth. Isn't it true that we sometimes hang on to things that are not the best for our health—mental, physical, or spiritual? Sometimes people contemplating divorce hang on to the relationship for the sake of the children, or because it's bound to get better, or for any number of reasons. But when they do let go, or decide to get counseling to see if it will help, when they take a step, it gets better.

The same is true with addiction. When we finally admit there is a problem and decide on our own to get help, we release that hellish grip of something outside of us. As we make that change we are accepting spirit. Whether or not we call it God or join a formal religion, we are listening to that voice of goodness inside, that voice that recognizes positive choices.

A wonderful television series called *Planet Earth* sometimes depicts different animals hunting each other. At first it seems a bit brutal, and yet the series reveals the food chain of which this hunting is part. At each new kill it shows the youngsters to whom the food is being brought. The baboon is bringing the bird back to its infants, the lion is bringing the baboon back to its cubs, and so the cycle goes. The point is that in nature the kill is usually for food.

We as a nation need to stand for peace. Perhaps we can learn from Mother Teresa who said she would never join an anti-war march, but that she would give her support to a peace rally. Perhaps we can learn to resolve arguments with words rather than fists. Little things add up to a big difference.

Peace is at the center of our very beings. When we light a candle for peace, we realize it is symbolic of the way peace is achieved. Peace begins within us, then moves out to our families, our communities, out to our country, and around the world.

Week 43
Release

So much in life has to do with just letting go and letting God. Someone cut out and pasted on my door a little cartoon that reads, "Good morning! This is God. I will be handling all your problems today. I will *not* need your help. So have a good day!" Part of Divine wisdom comes when we remember to turn to God for inspiration and help with challenges. Wisdom also comes from being thankful for everything that happens in our lives—It gives us more to be thankful for.

With each anniversary of 9/11 comes the lesson of release. What can be said about the world's race consciousness today when more than ten years ago two planes crashed into New York's Twin Towers? Security alerts are up, and I suppose that is a good thing, but what are we putting our attention on? Is it peace and harmony in the world? What would it be like to release all our fear and doubt about the safety of our nation and our world and concentrate on peace? Let us allow our race-conscious minds to focus on peace and harmony among nations and people of the world. Louise Hay says on one of her Power Cards,

> "I can release the past and forgive everyone."

On the back it continues,

> "I free myself and everyone in my life from old past hurts. They are free and I am free to move into new glorious experiences."

Very often there seems to be at least one person in our life we have trouble forgiving. For me it was Aunt Muriel. She was the youngest of my mother's six siblings and she never seemed to hold on to a job or a husband. When she was down and out, we always took her in. When we moved to California she hopped boxcars to get from Indiana to our door. My aunt was the first natural GPS; she tuned in to our house address with absolutely no effort. All during my high school years she lived at our house and shared my bedroom. As an adult, when I had the choice to be at a gathering with my aunt, I declined the invitation.

Shortly after I discovered Religious Science, we did an exercise to release old resentments. It was then I saw the absurdity of holding on to feelings about my aunt. I had excluded myself from many family events because of something she had little control over. The only person I ever punished was me. She was always thrilled whenever she saw me. Toward the end of her life, when she was suffering from Alzheimer's disease, I went to visit her quite often. Even though she wasn't always sure who I was, she still had that childlike excitement when seeing me.

There are many things we can allow to trouble us if we so choose—illnesses, jobs, relationships, finances—but the truth is, if we let God into the picture and partner with that incredibly intelligent and Creative Power behind everything, we can lay our troubles down at the altar of God.

A story by Paul Callory called "Something Inside Us Knows" in David Bruner's book, *All Is Well,* speaks of a man healing his body with prayer (188). Paul tells about going to the doctor for a scan of his lungs, and as he was lying in his room he could hear the doctors discussing how they would break some horrible news to a patient with cancer. Immediately he did a prayer treatment for this person, only to find out minutes later that he was the man they were talking about. The x-ray of his lungs showed several blood clots along with a large mass at the very bottom of his lung. The doctor suggested doing a needle biopsy. Paul felt the biopsy was something he didn't want to go through, and said he would go home and think about it. In response, the doctor told him that being in denial wouldn't help anything.

On the way home Paul did another prayer treatment on himself. He was more concerned about being told he was in denial than about the verdict of cancer. He knew in his heart of hearts that the tumor was not cancerous. He had a few more practitioners at his center do prayer treatments, and then the spiritual director of his center spoke with him and also did a treatment. Paul shared that he was feeling a little embarrassed about doing a treatment for himself when he was not a practitioner, but Rev. David said, "Paul, you are a practitioner; you just don't have a license yet."

Paul next visited a new doctor who ran an MRI and observed that the clots seemed a little smaller than in the last x-ray. He also said the tumor did not look cancerous. He wanted Paul to come back in a few months to check its progression. Not once in those two months did Paul think of himself as anything but healthy. When he did go back, there were no signs of clots and the tumor had vanished. As Ernest Holmes contends, "When we pray . . . we are healed."

Sometimes jobs release us; sometimes we release jobs. In that time between jobs, we can choose to let uncertainty overwhelm us, or we can trust the process. A new job means a new chapter in our lives, new friends, new opportunities, and new chances to grow. Someone at church once spoke of a man who turned down a job because he was told his current position was secure. Less than a month later he learned his company was preparing to shut down. He returned to the company he had turned down and although that job had been filled, a new and better position for more pay had come up, and he was told he would be the ideal person to fill the post. Life does have a way of unfolding perfectly when you release worry.

As for resentments, so often a person we are angry with has no clue we are mad and has gone on with life without a backward glance. I once had a student, divorced for over twenty-five years, who was still angry with her ex-husband for leaving her. "Release the past, move on to the greater achievements of the future," says the Optimist Creed.

Finances can also consume us. Concentrate on the money you do have and how you are able to pay your bills. They may seem high, but be grateful when you can pay them. Lay down the idea of lack and limitation, and say a prayer treatment. You may want to use one of my affirmative prayers:

> *I know I live in an abundant Universe and a loving and supportive God surrounds me. I partner with the Creative Intelligence of the Universe. I am connected to that Power. I live in an abundant world and have an abundance of friends, excellent health, and a wonderful place to live. And the truth is, I have more than enough money for my wants and needs. Money flows to me from a myriad of sources, both known and unknown. I am deeply thankful that this is so. I release these words to the Law of the Universe. I let go and let God, and so it is.*

You have laid your worry down, so step away from it and be anxious no more. Just as the farmer plants his seeds and doesn't go back and dig them up to see if they are growing, let go and trust the process. Today and every day, say, *I know I live in an abundant, peaceful Universe. A loving and supportive God surrounds me.*

There are many things we can allow to trouble us if we so choose, but the truth is, if we let God into the picture and partner with that incredibly Intelligent and Creative Power behind everything, we can lay it all down forever at the altar of God.

Week 44
Shift Your Perspective

When I was growing up I thought I had the most terrible parents ever. They made me tell them where I was going. I had to be home by a certain time every night. They checked to make sure I got my homework done; and I had to clean my room before I could go to the movies on Saturday. When I was young I thought they were tyrants. Now I view what they did for me then as good parenting. As an adult, I can look back with a shift in my perspective.

Shifting perspective brings to mind a number of issues. Some shifts are easy to make while others are not so obvious. For example, shifting to prayer treatment instead of complaining; or remembering the law of least resistance; or changing our attitudes; or remembering to forgive ourselves as easily as we forgive others. In general, changing our thinking changes our lives.

Complaining is a habit we sometimes fall into too easily: *Not another bill this month! If I get one more interruption, I'm going to scream! Why does a cold always seem to hit me every year?* Sound familiar? I know I'm guilty of sometimes forgetting to be thankful for everything I've gone through in my life. Every one of us is the right and perfect person precisely because we have been through those difficult chapters in our lives. The divorce from my first husband allowed me to realize I am a wonderful person who enjoys my own company. That split led me to find my spirituality and a wonderful new husband. Had that divorce not occurred I would not be experiencing Gary's caring presence. I might not even have found Religious Science or be the pastor I am today.

Finding the Center for Spiritual Living Tri-cities, where I serve as pastor, is a good example of shifting through prayer treatment. I had interviewed for two churches and each church chose another minister. Finally, I wrote a prayer treatment surrendering to Spirit. I said I knew there was a church meant for me, one that recognized the gifts I had to offer. I said I might not understand why events were turning out as they were but I surrender to Spirit, I trust the process. Right around this same time, the board of trustees in Kennewick, Washington, was treating for a minister with certain talents. And, lo and behold, it was a match. Prayer treatment instead of negative thinking . . . what a concept!

Another way to shift perspective is to use the law of non-resistance. Raymond Holliwell in his book, *Working with the Law*, comments,

> *Meekness, then, is that strength appropriated when you do not argue, when you do not become angry or boastful and proud, when you do not insist upon having your rights in a quarrelsome manner. Meekness is the steel of one's nature. It is enduring. Meekness is the strength by which you win an argument by refusing to argue.* (135)

James Thurber has a wonderful story, "The Unicorn in the Garden," that illustrates this point. A man wakes up, sees a unicorn in the garden, and tries to wake up his sleeping wife to show her, but she won't get up. He tries again and she starts getting annoyed. Finally, she regains consciousness enough to realize what he is telling her. She calls him a booby, and says they are going to put him in a booby hatch. He keeps insisting that there really is a unicorn in the garden. She thinks this is weird, calls the police, and a psychiatrist, and tells them to bring a straitjacket. When the medical attendants arrive she describes what her husband thinks he sees in the garden. The policeman then arrives, and the husband asks the officer if he's ever seen a unicorn. He says he hasn't seen a unicorn, that unicorns are mythical beasts. And the story ends with the psychiatrist's last lines: "I'm sorry, sir, but your wife is as crazy as a jay bird." So they take her away and shut her up in an institution. The husband then lives happily ever after.

Shift your perspective. We are always at choice as to how we respond to anything, and when we choose to respond with calm, the world is a kinder place. That goes for attitude, too. I have a coffee mug that says, "Attitude is a little thing that makes a big difference." And isn't it true when you go into a store where the clerk helps you, it can make all the difference in how you feel? Nordstrom's department store cites an example of a groom who needed same-day tailoring service on a suit for his wedding as his luggage had not arrived from the airport. Not only did they tailor his suit, but they delivered it to the church where he was being married.

As a teacher, I certainly didn't gloat over a student who earned a lower grade, but my attitude could be very open, honest, and caring as I discussed ways he could change his perspective and improve his grade.

Dennis Merritt Jones in a weekly email message from 2008, tells about waiting on the telephone for forty-five minutes to speak with the IRS to find out why his refund check had not come. We've all been there, waiting while they play "Raindrops Keep Falling on My Head" for the fiftieth time. He had hung up much sooner the other three times he had called. But while he was waiting this time, he stopped to do a prayer treatment. He treated for exactly the right person to answer the phone so when he was forced to wait he knew she must still be busy with another customer. When she finally answered, she was friendly, sympathetic, and helpful, and why not? After all, he had treated for the perfect situation to unfold.

A shift in perspective is sometimes needed when we blame ourselves for minor lapses. Have you noticed the person you are hardest on is often yourself? Candice Beckett, the president of Religious Science, wrote an article for *Creative Thought* magazine in which she recounted an incident that happened at her church. A client she had scheduled for a Monday appointment came in fifteen minutes late, berating herself for being late and apologizing profusely. It was all good, life happens, Candice let it go, the client let it go, they went on with the session, and all was fine. Tuesday, Candice arrived at church for a meeting six minutes late and was full of apologies. Although the client let it go, Candice berated herself, and continued berating herself after the client left. She could forgive the person on Monday for being late, but she lashed out at herself for the same lapse.

In the same issue of *Creative Thought,* March 2005, Tony Crapolicchio of the Decatur, Georgia, church talked about his introduction to Religious Science. It was summer. He had just released an addiction to drugs and was traveling to Florida on spring break. About fifty miles out of Atlanta the radio signals weakened to the point of no reception. Sitting in the back seat of the car he noticed a brightly colored magazine lying on the seat and asked his friend what it was. His friend said someone had given it to him, that it was some religious thing and that he should probably throw it out at the next stop. Tony was bored and with no radio to enjoy, he read the magazine cover to cover. Then he read it again.

By the time Tony got home from spring break he had read the magazine four more times. He decided he might as well check out the church, and, as luck would have it, there was a church a few blocks from his home. That was twenty years ago. Today Tony is a Religious Science minister and has spoken at Asilomar conferences in recent years. He believes consciousness is evolving, and he believes changing the consciousness of the world around us is very simple: practice the Science of Mind through teaching spiritual mind treatment. He points out there are more than six billion people on the planet today and that the world will change, one individual, one idea at a time. He believes in praying it forward. He suggests that if there are more than 10,000 subscribers to *Creative Thought* magazine, *and* if more people simply left their old magazines somewhere—in a dentist's office, on a park bench, in a friend's mailbox—perhaps someone like him will pick it up and read it and change his or her life. It is obviously up to each individual when he discovers the idea, and what he will do with it, but it is a step toward changing the race consciousness on earth to higher levels.

It is true that sometimes all it takes to change your life is to change your thinking. In Religious Science we believe that the Mind of God is everywhere. We each have an individual mind, but it is part of a greater whole. That creative force, that Mind, is behind everything in creation. So as God created out of Itself, we too can create through the use of our minds. Our thoughts create our reality. If this is so, then we should begin immediately to visualize our life as we want it to be.

When we look at the world through a different perspective, our focus can be drawn to things that really matter. Several friends and I went to a symposium, "Healing Journeys," a few years ago, for people who either were coping with cancer or had experienced cancer in the past. Many speakers talked about their cancer as being a blessing in disguise that helped them uncover what was most important in their lives. For many, a total life change helped them find a path to wellness. Others found it valuable to spend more time with loved ones and to set their affairs in order. Living with cancer gave them the opportunity to look at life from a different perspective.

All these people were saying yes to life, and isn't it just like Spirit to send you the perfect message at the right time? One such message came to me by e-mail one day. The subject line said, "The I Can't Funeral." It seems there was an elementary school teacher who was being evaluated, and on the day her evaluator came, she was doing a project with her students. She had them make a list of all the things they couldn't do. I can't kick a football and I can't play volleyball were just two items on some students' lists. The evaluator seemed puzzled by this negative project. The teacher collected all the lists and put them in a box that looked a bit like a small casket. Then the teacher borrowed a shovel from the custodian's cupboard and the class proceeded to the field outside. In about fifteen minutes, taking turns with the shovel, they had dug a three-foot hole where they buried the casket. The funeral then began. "Dearly beloved, we are gathered together to mourn the passing of I Can't. He is survived by his cousins, I Will Try, I'm Sure I Will, and Yes, I Can. He lies in this grave, no more to walk this planet. May he rest in peace." With that, the children went back to the classroom and celebrated with apple cider and popcorn, and then put up a tombstone in the room, honoring the death of I Can't. At any time during the semester when a student said, "I can't," the other students would point at the wall and chuckle.

A positive shift in perspective. Whether choosing prayer treatment instead of complaining; remembering to use the law of least resistance; remembering to be gentle with ourselves; or generally changing our thinking to change our lives, it is important to remember that yes, we can do it. We can if we think we can . . . when we remember, shift happens.

Week 45
Shoelaces and Ladybugs

Being tuned in to God is like being tuned in to the radio. When you are connected to a happy, positive station, you are happy and positive. When you are tuned in to a station that is sending out negativity, guess what? That's what you get. Everything that happens in life is cause and effect, the power of attraction, what you send out, you receive back.

To me, the phrase, "shoelaces and ladybugs" brings back happy childhood memories. I remember my father teaching me to tie my shoes and telling me the story of Br'er Fox chasing Br'er Rabbit around the bush and then Br'er Rabbit jumping into his hole. And I remember ladybugs were always a treat to see while helping my mom in the garden. Those are loving memories that bring a smile to my face. We can explore the more metaphysical lessons by taking a closer look at shoelaces and ladybugs.

What I find interesting about shoelaces is their ability to expand and contract to fit each person's foot. That to me is symbolic of the way God fits in to each person's life. Spirituality does not have to be the same for each person. And, just as shoelaces have the ability to pull things together, so we pull our lives together and can shape them in whatever ways we choose. We only need to realize it, recognize it, and use it.

Ladybugs are another one of those creatures that defy all odds when it comes to flight. They beat their wings eighty-five times a minute when they fly. Their life cycle is between four and six weeks long, although some Asian varieties can live for two to three years. Once they have transformed from larvae into ladybugs, it takes twenty-four hours for their spots to form. Aphids are a ladybug's favorite food, so their mothers will usually lay eggs near a nest of aphids. (I watched a movie about aphids in high school. I remember a munching sound as the ladybugs lunched on aphids but I don't know if the video camera just had a great sound system or if the munching sound was dubbed in.) I've learned that ladybugs emit a foul-smelling chemical that tastes awful, so predators won't eat them. They won't fly if the temperature is below fifty-five degrees. And they are the official state insect of Delaware, Massachusetts, New Hampshire, Ohio, and Tennessee.

Ladybugs help people without expecting anything in return. They seem to be there just to brighten up the world. They are a wonderful symbol of being in service to others, demonstrating Seva, or selfless service. Seva is the Sanskrit word for service to others. When we are spreading service to others we are spreading kindness and love, and we are expressing God. According to Mother Teresa,

> *Spread love everywhere you go; first of all in your own house. Give love to your children, to your wife or husband, to a next-door neighbor. . . Let no one ever come to you without leaving better and happier.*

Be the living expression of God's kindness; kindness in your face, kindness in your eyes, kindness in your smile, kindness in your warm greeting.
(thinkexist.com/quotation/spread_love_everywhere _you_go-first_of_all_in/14307.html)

So, let shoelaces be the reminder of your ability to expand or contract, to change as life changes, to make your life exactly as you desire it. Ernest Holmes in the text says,

> *The person who can throw himself with complete abandon into that Limitless Sea of Receptivity, having cut loose from all apparent moorings, is the one who will always receive the greatest reward.* (283)

And let ladybugs remind you that your clearest expression of God in action is when you give of yourself in selfless service. In his textbook on the teachings of Jesus, Ernest Holmes refers to the law of circulation from Matthew 10:8:

> *"Freely ye have received, freely give." When the law of circulation is retarded, stagnation results. It is only as we allow the Divine current to flow through us in and out that we really express life. The law of giving and receiving is definite. Emerson tells us to beware of holding too much good in our hands.*
>
> *When a man's thought rests entirely upon himself, he becomes abnormal and unhappy; but when he gives himself with enthusiasm to any legitimate purpose, losing himself in the thing which he is doing, he becomes normal and happy. Only as much life enters into us as we can conceive, and we conceive of life—in the larger sense—only when there is complete abandonment into it. Let the one who is sad, depressed, or unhappy find some altruistic purpose into which he may pour his whole being, and he will find a new inflow of which he has never dreamed.* (Science of Mind, 440)

Everything we do, every idea we generate, allows us to make our lives more purposeful. Raymond Charles Barker says in one of my favorite passages in *The Power of Decision,*

> Oliver Wendell Holmes wrote "Man's mind stretched to a new idea never goes back to its original dimensions." The more you are aware of the creative process, and your place in it, the larger the dimensions of your consciousness and the greater your use of right decisions to keep right on expanding. (87)

We can create our lives to be exactly as we want them to be. All we need are our thoughts and the ability to embody them. We need to plant the seeds in our subconscious minds, know it is done, and then let go and let God.

To give a radio analogy, when you are tuned to jazz, all you can expect on that station is jazz. When you are tuned to light rock, that's what you get. If you want country western music, you are not going to hear it on the classical station. As you tune in to the station you want, you can relax in the knowing that it will supply you with what you need. When you put an affirmative prayer into Mind, you can relax and know it will come about.

So much of our indecision and fear comes from worry. Raymond Charles Barker will tell you to make the decision and if it turns out to be the wrong choice, make another. Everything in our lives happens to us for a reason—good, or what we perceive as bad. Something may happen that appears to be bad, but days, weeks, years later, we realize it happened for a reason. Had it not happened, it would not have opened the door for something better. Anyone who is in a happy second marriage knows this. Every person we meet is there for a reason, a season, or a lifetime. What we must remember at a very deep level is that anything that happens isn't good or bad. It just is.

So while shoelaces remind us of the flexibility we have in life to meet any situation, we also must remember that God never gives us anything we can't handle. We have the ability to make something good out of whatever comes our way. And as ladybugs remind us to be kind to others and find ways to be of service, we grow to understand that this is God in expression and adds purpose to our lives. Love yourself, your family and friends, as Tom Reed, associate artistic director for Optimist Theatre, says, and "give every living creature you meet a smile" (Larson iii). Bubble over with laughter and the good in life. In doing these things, you are truly living.

Week 46
Simple Acceptance

Every so often I go through periods when I feel a little down, a little blue. Does that ever happen to you? There I was, lamenting all the friends and family I have living in other states, and how Gary and I had recently visited San Diego where the weather rarely is hotter than eighty-five in the summer, or colder than sixty-five in the winter. I was in the midst of a funk when I thought to myself: *Wait a minute; let's break out of this train of thought. What do I have to be grateful for right here, right now, right where I am?*

Immediately Gary and my family came to mind. Then my two little birds, Quimby and Emerson, came to mind. They can be annoying at times, but for the most part they are joyful little song meisters. I have a great house and I live in a location with low humidity in the summer. I am actually pretty darned content.

Simple Acceptance. So much can be learned from accepting things as they are, right here in this moment. Can you change anything that happens after this present moment? If you have an accident, can anything change the fact that you had an accident? You can wrack your brain thinking of all you could have done to avoid the accident, but the fact is, it happened.

I was working at the Broadway department store one year when my mother showed up and in a frazzled state ranted about her purse that had just been stolen. Apparently, two people on a motorcycle came right at her and when she stepped back, hands in the air, totally startled, the second man on the motorcycle reached out and grabbed her handbag. When my dad heard about the incident he said, "You should have put your umbrella through his wheel." Well, it wasn't raining, and Dad wasn't there, and it was a very harrowing and confusing experience for my mother. After an accident you may discover what you might do to prevent a second accident, but you can't deny the fact that the event happened the way it happened.

What about those times when something occurs that is not your fault; some act by your dog, your kids, or your spouse, which makes it impossible for you to simply accept what happened? Do you let them get away with doing things they shouldn't be doing? How does this differ from being a doormat, letting people walk all over you? The bottom line is to respond, in the moment, in a calm manner, rather than have a knee-jerk reaction. Much of the attitude we receive from others is a direct response to the annoyance we have displayed. What we are sending out, we are getting back.

Before we got married, Gary used to take care of his room-mate's daughter, Chule, while his roommate was working the night shift. He made sure the young lady was ready every morning before he gave her a ride to high school. One morning Chule made Gary late for work. He told her that the next day that if she wasn't ready when he had to leave, she would be walking to school.

The next morning came; she wasn't ready; Gary left her behind. When her mom came home from the night shift Chule was still there. She told her mom what had happened and asked for a ride, but her mother said, "No, you can walk; you will just be late. Gary told you if you were ready on time, he would have dropped you off." Simple acceptance: these are the rules; you need to follow them.

During the school year I usually spend a few hours a day tutoring for the local school district. What I find to be the case time after time is that a student who by all accounts is a terror in the classroom, is quite reasonable when working alone with me. However, in a classroom of thirty-five kids, five of whom exhibit disruptive behavior, I can imagine that a teacher might not just silently accept what is going on. The truth is, however, the teacher is accepting the fact that there needs to be a new experience for that child. While we can't change the exact moment we are in, we can plan for the future.

We cannot continue acting in the same manner when a problem exists and expect change. Simple acceptance may merely be the acknowledgment of needing change. Sometimes acceptance is uncomplicated, as the Serenity Prayer reminds us:

> *God grant me the serenity to accept*
> *the things I cannot change;*
> *Courage to change the things I can;*
> *and wisdom to know the difference.*
> (brainyquote.com/quotes/r/reinholdin100884.htm)

Now and then, simple acceptance means owning that we are good enough just as we are. Too often we are hardest on ourselves, belittling our appearance, rejecting compliments, hitting ourselves over the head for silly mistakes that possibly no one even noticed but ourselves. I've learned I just need to say thank you when I get a compliment, instead of pointing out that I got my outfit on sale, or that it didn't take any time at all to prepare a meal. Try it; just say thank you. Accept.

Accept the fact that we are all perfect, whole, and complete just as we are. We can make a decision to change things that we would like to be different, but we don't *have* to change a thing. Dr. David Walker, past president of International Centers for Spiritual Living, wrote a book entitled, *You Are Enough*. He prompts us to remember that, just as we are, we are each valuable.

We are the ones who most often refuse to accept ourselves as we are. Simple acceptance is easier to achieve when recognizing that the creative Intelligence of God *wants* us to have all the good we are willing to receive.

Sometimes simple acceptance requires being mindful of things that might happen, covering all bases, planning ahead. Sometimes acceptance means ascertaining all the facts, realizing the truth in a situation. Most of all, simple acceptance comes from trusting that the highest and best will always turn up. Sometimes it takes a shift, but as the saying goes, "Shift happens."

Someone you love dies, a divorce takes place, you move to a new location, you change jobs . . . with any new situation comes some adjustment. Wayne Dyer's deck of inspirational cards advises us to "Believe in Universal Timing":

> *You must believe in a Universe that's created and guided by Intelligence greater than your ego—a Universe where there can be no accidents. When an idea's time has come, it can't be stopped. And the reverse of this is true: An idea whose time hasn't come can't be created.*

You may be looking for a new job and go to an interview, but not be hired. You might be disappointed, but when the next interview comes along, and you get that new and better job, you realize everything happened for a reason.

Forrest Gump is a perfect example of a man who understood simple acceptance. He rarely worried about a thing, but the best always happened for him. "Life is like a box of chocolates; you never know what you're gonna get," was a viewpoint of simple acceptance that what is to be, is to be. I think that line could be changed to say, "You never know *exactly* what you are going to get."

When we do affirmative prayer, we put into Mind what it is we desire, then we let go and know the highest and best will manifest. Simple acceptance, acceptance with gratitude, no matter the outcome, brings the contentment of having even more to be thankful for.

Week 47
Something Spicy
This Way Comes

Spirituality is our choice. It is ours for the asking. We may have been raised in a religion that doesn't work for us but that does not mean we are not spiritual; it means we haven't yet found the right fit. When you find that special something that does feel like home, you reap your spiritual harvest.

A Ray Bradbury novel, *Something Wicked This Way Comes,* is the inspiration for this chapter, "Something Spicy This Way Comes." The book carries a theme of acceptance. There are old characters wishing to be young, and young characters wishing to be old, and the story describes what happens to them when they try to be something they are not.

We don't believe in the term "sin" in Religious Science. We believe people may make poor decisions and are punished by those decisions, not by God. It's all about cause and effect, the power of attraction, and understanding that what you are sending out, you are getting back.

So often when we are pretending to be something we are not, we make our poorest decisions. Do we look at ourselves honestly? Ernest Holmes professes

> One should analyze himself, saying, "Do I look at myself from a standpoint of restriction? Do I see life limited to the eternal round of getting up in the morning, eating, going to work, coming home, going to bed, sleeping, getting up again and so on?" Break the bonds of apparent necessity and see life as one continuous expression of the Infinite Self, and as this conception gradually dawns upon the inner thought, something will happen in the outer conditions to relieve the greater demands of necessity. Free yourself forever from the thought that God may be pleased by a life of sacrifice, that the world is any better because of your misery, or righteousness is more perfectly expressed through poverty than abundance. Know that the greater abundance of every good thing which you are bringing out in your life, the more perfectly you are satisfying the Divine Urge within you. ANYTHING YOU CAN DREAM OF is not too great for you to undertake, if it hurts no man and brings happiness and good into your life. (Science of Mind, 288)

So let your words include the positive self-talk that reaps a glorious spiritual harvest. When we aren't honest with ourselves, problems pile up. Think for a moment about your home computer. If you never upgrade and your hard drive piles up with all your downloads from years past, your computer may start to slow down, and eventually may crash. Apply that same analogy to how we think. If we never upgrade our thoughts, and allow everyone around us to download their programs onto us, we too can slow down and eventually crash by becoming argumentative or sick or having an accident. Psychologist Dr. Phil McGraw refers to this as a life of self-betrayal.

I relate to this computer analogy in a couple of ways. Until I was forty-four, too many people downloaded their programs onto me. Then I discovered Religious Science and soon realized no one was dumping things on me without my permission. I learned I had the power to choose to live life differently. The ancientness of my computer was brought to my attention when Gary and I first began dating. Very quickly we upgraded my Packard Bell computer to something new and more workable. That was the birth of Internet capability at my condo and another lesson in letting go of the old to make room for the new.

Many people looking for a new relationship after a significant other has died or moved on realize they need to clean out their closets to make room for someone new in their lives. Opening your heart, clearing out the old, and expressing yourself authentically will welcome new loved ones into your life. It's also important to remember to do the things you want to do and not let other people's opinions get in your way. Dr. Naomi Remen in her book, *Kitchen Table Wisdom* tells the story of her mother's eightieth birthday:

> Naomi asked, "Mom, what do you want to do on your 80th birthday?" She replied, "Climb the Statue of Liberty." Naomi said, "I think there's an elevator." Her mom replied, "No, I want to climb the steps." She had seen the Statue of Liberty on the outside when she was a child of nine, newly arrived from Russia. There were 342 steps and they climbed them three steps at a time, pausing for her mother to catch her breath. It took them six hours, and, when they

were up to the last six steps, her mother queried,
"Why couldn't we have done these last steps first?"

In closing Rachel says, "In thinking of this story now,
I remember all the times that I, too, have resented
the climb, the amount of living needed to gain the
precious understanding to know how to live well.
And how important it is in the struggle for freedom
from the old ways not to be limited by style or self-
expectations or to worry about what others think.
To be willing to do the really important things any
way you can, even three steps at a time." (173)

Just think of that eighty-year-old woman who did something so many people thought she would not be able to do. What do you long to do? Travel? Reunite with an old friend? Mend a relationship?

I talked with a neighbor after my mother died who told me she finally spoke with her daughter after being estranged from her for ten years. She discovered her daughter was in the Air Force and would soon be going to Iraq. She learned she had an eight-year-old granddaughter and was going to meet her soon. This brought home the importance of not missing out on the joys available to us by refusing to mend troubled relationships.

"Something Spicy This Way Comes," can remind us to take pleasure in the spice of life. I believe life should be a balance of enjoyable work, a healthy spiritual life, and a healthy personal life. If you are at all like me, you may find yourself concentrating mostly on the first two. But the last area, the healthy personal life, is where the spice is. Remember to nurture yourself with a satisfying personal life. And one more thing, always remember it is never too late to do something you've always wanted to do.

You are good enough; you are the perfect age and the perfect size. You are perfect, whole, and complete, just as you are.

Week 48
The Calm Within the Storm

The old saying, "It's the calm before the storm," refers to a phenomenon that happens in the Midwest before many thunder or windstorms. This chapter, however, is about the calm *within* the storm. The very center of a cyclone or hurricane, the eye, is peaceful and quiet and without rain. It is usually warm and is surrounded by a wall of heavy rain and debris, yet the center is calm.

This same state of calm remains in the enlightened being when havoc occurs. It is in the person who has learned to respond rather than react. It is the person who turns within to meditate who maintains a peace within.

How does the ability to sustain this sense of peace help us in our daily lives? At the office, remaining calm in the presence of agitation helps the befuddled person think straight. When you don't pick up negative energy, you do not become enmeshed in drama. Often siblings or other family members love to push your buttons. If you refuse to take the bait, arguments easily dissipate because there's no one left with whom to quarrel. If someone is angry and you do not respond with your own volatile anger, the situation will not escalate. You are the calm in the eye of the storm.

Every person on this planet has his or her own personal power. We each have the power to create our own life experiences. That Power, that inner being, is connected to God. Esther and Jerry Hicks address this thought with one of their cards from a deck on life's daily messages. The front of the card reads,

I am becoming consciously aware of my inner being.

The back of the card states,

> *We refer to that Non-Physical You as your inner being or your source. It is not important what you call that Source of Energy, or Life Force, but it is important that you are consciously aware of when you are allowing a full connection to it and when you are restricting it in some way.*

Are you debating over some issue in your life? Are you not sure whether to move to a new location, take a different job, end a relationship, or start a new one? Perhaps you are being guided by that still small voice residing within you, but you haven't yet made your mind up to move forward. Whatever it is, if you are still not sure what to do, try affirmative prayer. Taking a new step is often very hard, but if you never take the step, you'll never be able to experience that new and positive change.

When we came to Washington State, Gary and I didn't know what to expect. I knew there was a wonderful new church community, but I didn't know how I would handle cold weather. Gary looked at the map and said, "Where the heck is Kennewick?" But we made a change. We stepped out in faith, knowing God would always be there to guide us, if we listened. We are so happy that we took the step. We are so blessed to be in a loving community, where we make a difference in the lives of those around us.

Being the calm within the storm is especially helpful when responding to disappointments. So often there is a silver lining that comes with realizing things are not good or bad; they just are, as this story depicts:

> *Years ago in Scotland, the Clark family had a dream. Clark and his wife worked and saved, making plans for their nine children and themselves to travel to the United States. It had taken years, but they had finally saved enough money and had gotten passports and reservations for the whole family on a new liner to the United States.*
>
> *The entire family was filled with anticipation and excitement about their new life. However, seven days before their departure, a dog bit the youngest son. The doctor sewed up the boy but hung a yellow sheet on the Clarks' front door. Because of the possibility of rabies, they were being quarantined for fourteen days.*
>
> *The family's dreams were dashed. They would not be able to make the trip to America as they had planned. The father, filled with disappointment and anger, stomped to the dock to watch the ship leave— without the Clark family. The father shed tears of disappointment and cursed both his son and God for their misfortune.*
>
> *Five days later, the tragic news spread throughout Scotland—the mighty Titanic had sunk. The unsinkable ship had sunk taking hundreds of lives with it. The Clark family was to have been on that ship, but,*

because a dog had bitten the son, they were left behind in Scotland.

When Mr. Clark heard the news, he hugged his son and thanked him for saving the family. He thanked God for saving their lives and turning what he had felt was a tragedy into a blessing. Although we may not always understand, all things happen for a reason. (http://titanic3.tripod.com/stories.html)

So it is important not to get involved in labeling a situation good or bad. It just is; it has its reason for happening in our lives and it serves us to remain calm and remember this. Ernest Holmes has a treatment for calmness in *The Science of Mind* textbook. The last few lines read,

> *There is no worry, irritation or agitation. I am sustained in a deep inner calm. Spirit flows through me and is never obstructed by anything unlike Itself. There is no overaction, no inaction, nor is there any wrong action of Spirit within me. Its action is complete, harmonious and perfect. Everything that does not belong to Pure Spirit is washed away.* (255)

The calm within the storm helps us know that life always turns out exactly as it should, unfolding in Divine right order. When we do a treatment or say an affirmative prayer we put into words that which we wish to have come about, with conviction and an inner sense of knowing. Then we let it go, we trust the process. So often, I will do a prayer treatment about something, maybe a problem I have at school or a writer's block I'm having while preparing a talk, and later in the week I'll be amazed at how well things are going. Then I remember: My prayer has been answered. When I let the problem go, guess what? God responded. From *The Science of Mind* textbook again,

We should take time every day to see life as we wish it to be, to make a mental picture of our ideal. We should pass this picture over to the Law and go about our business, with a calm assurance that on the inner side of life something is taking place. There should not be any sense of hurry or worry about this, just a calm, peaceful sense of reality. Let the Law work through, and express Itself in, the experience. There should be no idea of compulsion. We do not have to make the Law work; it is Its nature to work. In gladness then, we should make known our desires, and in confidence we should wait upon the Perfect Law to manifest through us. (271-272)

Life holds many pleasant possibilities for each of us and we must focus on the outcome. What are the attributes you want in a job? What qualities do you desire in a friend or mate? If you are seeking peace or harmony or trust, what are you sending out?

Meditation is a way to practice detachment from the outer world as you go within. Set aside some time each day to just be silent. It's amazing what will happen when we take the time to just be. This means to set aside all of the "doing," and just be with the silence. The question may arise, "What do I do when I want to quiet down but my mind won't cooperate?" If there is struggle in releasing the chatter, try focusing on a candle flame; or sit and listen to some Native American flute music or other gentle music with no words to it, something that allows you to merely listen to the sound. The idea is to detach yourself from everyday thought.

Detachment allows us to get into the zone, and is actually the prerequisite. Wayne Dyer talks about this as well, but he calls it the "gap." In *Getting in the Gap*, Dyer talks about getting into the gap in meditation where we enter a sacred space and commune with God. He likens our thoughts to a pond, and the chatter that goes on there is like the wind on the water at its surface. All that surface chatter is like the whitecaps that form on the surface, but when you go below, the water is calm. This is similar to our thoughts during meditation. It's said that we have over 60,000 thoughts in a day. Most are disconnected and jumbled, so to find the space between the thoughts, to find and get into the gap, is meditation.

Meditation allows us to be that calm within the storm. Practicing the awareness of peace is a great dress rehearsal for the storm that life sometimes becomes, and while we may not always control what happens around us, we can always control how we respond to the situation. Some call this ability being centered.

Remember to stay centered no matter what may be occurring around you. Remember to be the calm within the storm so as to reap your silver linings. As Ernest Holmes says about giving a spiritual mind treatment, "There is no irritation, frustration, or resentment in my life. Any sense of inner agitation is now wiped away, and in its place there comes a warm sense of my oneness in essence and experience with all the good there is. The center of my being is understanding and intelligence. I am calm, poised and at peace with the world." (*Science of Mind,* 249)

Week 49
The Delicate Art of
Mind Reading

We all live in the present moment, and we all have an incredible gift. We have the gift of deciding what our lives will be like each and every day. It doesn't matter whether we wake up in the morning and say it's a horrible day or wake up and say it's a glorious day—either way, we are right. Whether we win the lottery or sit down to pay bills, we are *always* the ones who decide to be happy with our circumstances, or ticked off. If it is angst we choose to dwell on, guess what? We find ourselves with more to worry about. So be grateful for each and every experience, even the occasional fender bender; it wakes us up and allows us to remember to be more focused in the present moment.

This chapter, "The Delicate Art of Mind Reading," was inspired by Malcolm Gladwell's book, *Blink*. He cites a study of psychologists who learned to read peoples' faces and emotions by the expressions they make. Sometimes a person's expression might show for just a fleeting second, but his theory is that all human beings, no matter what country they are from, no matter their gender or ethnic background, use these same expressions. This may be why we sometimes meet someone and make an instant intuitional assessment of that person. But what we are seeing is only a thin slice of what the person is truly like. First impressions might be good for our safety's sake, but they can also close the door on getting to know a person.

How can this delicate art of mind reading apply to relationships? Suppose that a person says something that hurts your feelings, but you don't tell him or her your feelings are hurt; you just walk away and vow that it will be a long time before you see that person again. How hard would it have been to air your real feelings in a calm and factual way? Perhaps you misinterpreted what your friend said to you. Responding honestly may have helped you understand what was meant by the remark.

How many times have you heard, "I'm not a mind reader"? My mother had a funny and somewhat snide remark for the numerous times my father would ask where his tie was. She would say, "It's hanging on the nail in the middle of my back." The only mind we should ever need to read is our own.

> An Indian furniture dealer wanted to expand the line
> of furniture in his store so he decided to go to Paris
> to see what he could find. After arriving in Paris he
> met with some manufacturers and finally selected
> a new line of furniture that he thought would sell
> back home in India.
>
> To celebrate the new acquisition, he decided to visit
> a pub. As he sat down to enjoy his wine, a very attrac-
> tive young lady came to his table, asked him some-

*thing in French (which he did not understand),
and motioned toward the chair. He invited her to sit
down, tried speaking to her in Hindi, Punjabi, and
English, but she did not know any of these languages.
So, after a couple of minutes of trying to communicate, he took a napkin and drew a picture of a wine
glass and showed it her. She nodded, and he ordered
a glass of wine for her.*

*After sitting together at the table for a while he drew
a picture of a plate of food on another napkin, and
she nodded. They left the pub and found a quiet cafe
that featured a small group playing romantic music.
They ordered dinner, after which he drew another
picture, this one of a couple dancing. She nodded,
and they danced until the band was packing up.
They went back to their table and the young lady
took a napkin and drew a picture of a bed . . . and
. . . would you believe it? To this day, the Indian has
no idea how she figured out he was in the furniture
business. (emmitsburg.net › My Little Sister's Jokes
› List of Groaner Jokes)*

The gentle art of mind reading.

In some ways we could consider our subjective mind a mind
reader, or, perhaps more accurately, a thought reader, because
what we think about, comes about. Ernest Holmes tells us that

*one cannot be a good student of the Science of Mind
who is filled with fear and confusion. He must keep
himself in a state of equilibrium, in a state of poise,
peace and confidence . . . in a state of spiritual
understanding. (Science of Mind, 160)*

So I am now changing the phrase "The delicate art of mind
reading" to "The peaceful, confident art of intuition."

Malcolm Gladwell's book cites an example of a policeman chasing three teenage gang members. Two jumped over a fence and got away. One remained on the street. As the officer drew closer he told the young man to stop. His partner repeated, "Stop, stop, stop." The young man turned slightly and reached into his pants, and the officer immediately thought, gun. He was poised and ready to shoot, but his intuition told him to wait. The young man did pull out a gun, but at waist level he dropped it. The boy was arrested, but not killed (239-241).

This officer used the peaceful, confident art of intuition. Stopping to tune in for just a minute in any challenging situation allows you to resolve it with a spiritual solution. Dr. Wayne Dyer explains exactly that in his book, *10 Secrets for Success and Inner Peace:*

> *Any problem can be resolved with a spiritual solution. A Course in Miracles suggests that you don't have a problem; you merely think you do. The opening lines of the Torah, as well as Genesis in the Bible state, "God Created the Heaven and Earth," and later, "And all that God created was good." If you interpret those words literally, it's quite clear that problems are impossible. If God created everything, and all that God created was good, bad does not exist. (85)*

Be grateful for each and every experience, even those that are not on your top ten list, as they are the very ones that wake us up and allow us to remember to be more focused in the present moment. And when you are, you can practice the peaceful, confident art of intuition. Say to yourself, "I practice the peaceful, confident art of intuition." And so it is.

Week 50
The Sounds of Silence

The melody of life is made up of all the people, places, and events that have shaped us into who we are today.

When I was in high school, my best friend and I took home white rats for the summer, and what do you think we named them? Simon and Garfunkel. It's a bit ironic that the title of this chapter should be the title of a song by the same artists. Let's look at some of the facts that went into writing the song, "The Sounds of Silence," and some of the implied meanings, and what the song represents on a metaphysical level.

Simon and Garfunkel began singing together in high school as fifteen-year-olds. "The Sound of Silence" with only acoustical guitar accompaniment was first released as part of an album in 1964. It bombed, and Simon and Garfunkel split up. But according to the official website, Columbia Records producer Tom Wilson, unbeknownst to Simon and Garfunkel, added an electrical guitar and rhythm section to the track and rereleased it. It was a smashing success, and the duo came back together.

Simon had written the lyrics very slowly, about one line a day over a period of six months. The words were about man's lack of communication with his fellow man. The song was then picked up for use in the movie, *The Graduate*. Here, the lyrics refer to silence as a cancer that eats away at people who never tell the truth, and implied that if people in the movie had been honest and not afraid to talk, the numerous messy scenarios would not have occurred. Problems must be solved with honesty (Songfacts.com).

When you are silent, you are usually alone, and for some people that can be scary. One of the greatest gifts after my divorce was learning that I enjoy my own company. I grew to be comfortable in the silence of my own little condo. And that's when my new love walked into my life. Coincidentally, Gary had just come to a similar realization when he met me. Doesn't it feel good when you can sit and enjoy silence with a friend or loved one and feel comfortable without talking?

You can be in a crowd of people and still feel lonely. But alone, sitting in silence, can be a full and powerful experience. It's all in your perspective. There is a Buddhist tale about bugs running frantically around in a glass bowl looking for a way out. One of the bugs, however, stops for a moment, leans back against the bowl and says, "Wow, nice bowl."

It's all in your perspective. In Religious Science we embrace the belief that silence is powerful because so often when we go within and meditate we come up with some of our best ideas. Let's look at Simon and Garfunkel's song from a metaphysical perspective. The song speaks of silence being a friend and leaving remnants from those times we were in meditative silence.

Very often, if I meditate on a situation that has occurred in my life, particularly at night, and I know I have a decision to make, I will wake in the morning with the answer clearly etched in my mind. The visioning has taken place. Ernest Holmes writes

The intelligence by and through which we perceive that there is a Spiritual Presence and an Infinite Mind in the Universe, constitutes our receptivity to it, and decides Its flow through us (*Science of Mind*, 41)

In other words, when I believe in the power of my mind to demonstrate what is right and perfect for me, and when I allow that good to flow through me, I am delighted with the outcome.

The song also speaks of the times we try to ignore people and situations, and keep our feelings bottled up inside of us. This is what happens when there is a lack of communication or when we have a wonderful idea that we sit on and do nothing about. The greatest gift at times is when another person urges us on. I took a modern dance class in junior high school. I had been dancing my heart out, thinking I was doing a good job, but at the end of the semester all the kids in class, except for me and a girl who had broken her arm, went to the multipurpose room to put on a performance for the school. The girl with the broken arm and I sat in the locker room alone during the performance. As an adult and a drama teacher, I always try to include everyone who wants to participate. I can see now with absolute clarity that the dance teacher could have let one of us work the record player and the other work the lights. A good lesson here is to communicate; speak up for yourself and others. Don't be afraid to disturb the silence for a friend, for yourself, or for a good cause.

Messages are written everywhere in life. When we pay attention, those sounds of silence become powerful. Make the time to go within and connect with Spirit and treasure those moments of clarity instead of wondering where you'll ever find the time to get everything done.

Brother John entered the "Monastery of Silence" and the abbot said, "Brother, this is a silent monastery; you are welcome here as long as you like, but you may not speak until I direct you to do so."

Brother John lived in the monastery for five years before the abbot said to him, "Brother John, you have been here five years now; you may speak two words." Brother John said, "Hard bed."

"I'm sorry to hear that," the abbot said. "We will get you a better bed." After another five years, the abbot again called Brother John. "You may say another two words, Brother John."

"Cold food," said Brother John, and the abbot assured him that the food would be better in the future. On his fifteenth anniversary at the monastery, the abbot again called Brother John into his office. "Two words you may say today."

"I quit," said Brother John.

"It is probably best; you've done nothing but complain since you got here" (Danggoogjokes.com).

Metaphysically, the sounds of silence can also translate to mean not forgiving someone. When we fail to forgive and instead linger over a "story" that happened to us, fretting for years and years, it is like a slow poison killing our joy in life.

The sounds of silence can also represent staying in one place and refusing to make a decision to move forward, perhaps out of the fear of not knowing what our lives would be like after the decision is made. Caroline Reynolds, in her book *Spiritual Fitness*, shares

Remember that a parachute cannot open while you are still standing on the ground. But the moment you make that bold jump out of your old comfort zone your parachute will instantly unfurl and help you to sail along. (41)

Meditation that allows you to quiet a chattering mind, to connect with God and listen to the voice of Divine inspiration, is the finest sound of silence. As Anais Nin says so eloquently,

And the day came when the risk it took to remain tight in the bud was more painful than the risk it took to blossom. (brainyquote.com)

Listen to the melodies of life. Step out into untried territory. Be present and fully involved in living. And always allow time to go into the silence and listen to the voice of wisdom from within, the voice of God's inspiration.

Week 51
There Shall Come
Gentle Rains

When I'm standing in line at the grocery store and get up to the cashier, I sometimes realize, with vivid clarity, that I've become my mother. I remember standing in line with her and waiting for fifteen minutes until it was our turn for the clerk to wait on us. Then, even though she had plenty of time earlier, my mother would spend another ten minutes looking for her credit card. I would think to myself, *Why didn't she look for the card while we were waiting in line?* Now I sometimes find myself doing the same thing. It's remarkable what gets handed down through the generations. It has nothing to do with genetics, of course, so it is interesting to see myself doing things I said I would never do.

"There Will Come Soft Rains" is the title of a Ray Bradbury story set in the distant future after war has destroyed a population. As the story opens, mechanical mice have emerged from a wall in a house to perform daily cleaning duties. Automated voices tell the time and schedule for the day. On the garage door are charred outlines of the human beings who died in a nuclear blast. The only things that remain are robot devices and sprinklers that operate on a timer. The soft rains referred to here are the water droplets from the automated sprinkler. Bradbury is gently saying to be mindful of the advances we make through modern technology. Soft rains refer also to the cleansing process of time and what nature may do to heal.

Life appears to be a cycle. In nature we see the changing of the seasons. The climate follows a pattern to match the seasons. Every spring we see the buds of new flowers and leaves sprouting on branches. Sunrises and sunsets; waves ebbing and flowing; birds migrating in winter; salmon swimming upstream. Nature has a way of maintaining balance.

From time to time natural disasters occur—a forest fire, or a flood. When we are in the midst of such a calamity it is difficult to see any blessing that may materialize, especially if our home or possessions are destroyed. But after the fire, in the ashes new seedlings grow. The pinecone bursts open in the heat to generate new life. People come together after disasters, and are thankful that their lives are spared. Life is a cycle, and when something in nature is used up, something else shows up to fill the vacuum.

A one-act play by Thornton Wilder, *The Long Christmas Dinner,* is about one hundred years of Christmas dinners in the same house. Throughout the story people are born into and die out of this one family. Wilder points out similarities and differences experienced by the family over the years. One recurring line is, "Look at that branch, it's encircled with ice; you almost never see that." He is pointing out how much remains the same throughout time.

Sometimes events happen in life to complete a cycle. We lose an old job so a better one may come along. We release an old relationship to allow a new one to take its place. It helps when we remember that our thoughts create our reality and that our thoughts are also a cycle—a cycle of cause and effect.

Time heals. The events that occur in our lives are the milestones we look back on. We can sometimes laugh at them, no matter how catastrophic they may have seemed at the time, but we always learn from them. When we reach those challenging moments in life and overcome them, there is growth. God never gives us more than we can handle. Poet Edna St. Vincent Millay reminds us, "Those eyes that are the most lovely are not those that have cried the least tears" ("To a Young Girl"). When you've experienced a moment of challenge and come through it, the rest can only be better.

One Sunday I woke up early and discovered there was no coffee in the house, so I walked up to Starbucks only to find it was closed. Several employees were outside, but the person with the key had overslept. I thought, *Things happen for a reason. I know! I was meant to go to 7-11 for a lottery ticket!* When I arrived at 7-11 their fancy coffee machine was down, so I bought a cup of inexpensive coffee and went home. Later, at church, I discovered we had no service coordinator for the day. Now, at this point I could have become perturbed over all these morning mishaps, but instead I decided to go with the flow, and to trust that someone else would get the opportunity to help out. As it turned out, everything worked out smoothly. As people arrived and they were asked to help, they seemed delighted to lend a hand. There are no accidents.

Occasionally, into our lives some rain must fall, but our attitude about those events can make them seem as either a violent storm or a gentle drizzle. What garden doesn't benefit from a little rainfall? Likewise, we human beings benefit from the stones placed in our way; we grow as we uncover them. Raymond Holliwell in *Working with the Law* says this in his chapter on the law of non-resistance:

> To live wisely one must be strong and positive,
> though righteously meek. Such strength is not
> measured in physical brawn and muscle, but in mind

and spirit . . . Meekness is the strength by which you
win an argument by refusing to argue (135).

Refuse to buy into the belief that there is a certain way something *should* happen. Garth Brooks has a song entitled, "Unanswered Prayers" in which he goes to a high school reunion only to meet the girl he was once in love with. He remembers how he'd spent many a night praying for God to make her his own. Now, in looking back, he sees his current wife and his current family, and he thanks God for unanswered prayers.

There are things we wish for that may not necessarily be in our best interest, yet we think we desperately need them. Sometimes when we pray, our subconscious minds sabotage us. In our heart of hearts, in our minds, we are not truly seeing the demonstration as possible, so our wish doesn't come about. And what happens when life takes a detour, and those challenging moments occur? We have the opportunity to practice our creativity. In fact, challenges keep our lives from being routine and boring. Raymond Charles Barker, in *The Power of Decision*, states,

> *Routined living does not make for happiness. It may*
> *create efficiency, but it is an efficiency that is dull and*
> *monotonous . . . . We have the false belief that order*
> *and efficiency give us greater ease, and thus, without*
> *realizing it, we have made ease the end goal of living,*
> *which it is not.* (127)

In other words, when we can meet those unexpected moments with creativity and a mellow attitude, we may discover that what we perceived to be a challenge was really a blessing in disguise.

One day in my former life as a high school drama teacher, I was contemplating the blessings in disguise that were occurring in my life. I was working with three other teachers to put on a musical but I taught in three different classrooms on opposite ends of the campus. A remodeling was taking place on campus, so jackhammers were making a constant racket. These blessings really were disguised. Although it took a lot of coordinating, I realized it really was a lighter load to produce a play shared among four people. And, as the classrooms were far apart, I was getting exercise walking on the job even while I was concerned about not getting to the gym as often as I used to. Not only that, but all those jackhammers were preparing the grounds for beautiful new rooms on campus the next year.

So into our lives a little rain must fall, but if we are mindful, we remember to appreciate the rainbow that often comes along as well. The bottom line is that God's Divine right order doesn't always coincide with our concept of what that order should be.

My mother had a friend whose son was a lawyer and had married while he was just finishing his last year of law school. He and his wife had planned to wait for a few years before they had children, but guess what? They got pregnant just a few months into their marriage. They were in love and they took it in stride. He finished his law degree, got a job, and also started his own practice. Just a few months into his new career he had a terrible car accident and was paralyzed from the waist down. The accident was a terrible one, but he was alive and still able to function. If the couple hadn't had their baby when they did, they would never have had children naturally.

We are always at choice as to how we respond to any situation. When we have the presence of mind to go within and ask for direction, a solution always comes about. Allowing events to happen without reacting out of fear or anger, and realizing there are no accidents, we come to understand that our lives are fuller as we creatively work through challenging moments. We simply need to remember that the outcome is often better than we ever could have imagined, especially when we partner with God.

When those gentle rains flow into your life, accept them as such—gentle. Your reaction can keep them from turning into raging storms. It's all about responding to the world around you with no resistance, accepting the present moment with grace. Be conscious of where your attention is placed. Make sure your awareness is sited on the wonderful blessings we all are in each other's lives, and celebrate the unique gifts we bring to the world.

Week 52
Wake Up the Kid in You

"Live Your Second Childhood," is the title of a card from the deck, *The Life Lift-off Cards* by Michael Beckwith. The card reads,

> *Your life began in the heart and mind of the Infinite. Mentally relive the days when as a child you ran free, when there were Infinite possibilities of what you could feel, accomplish and see in the world. Allow for the energy of your remembered freedom to thunder through you, and you will free yourself from the false obstacles your adult life has put in your path.*

What obstacles do you perceive to have in your world right now, in this exact moment? Could it be lack of funds, a troubled relationship, problems at work, an illness or lack of mobility, or are you finally at a place in life where you feel totally relaxed and free from allowing any person or situation to cloud your peace of mind? If you are at that relaxed and enlightened state already, let it keep thundering through you.

Let's consider financial conditions. What was your childhood like in the money arena? I grew up with parents from two very different worlds. My mother was born to Methodist missionaries in India. There were six children in her family and her father died when she was three. My grandfather on my father's side owned the first Ford dealership in Indianapolis. In my more immediate family, my father was highly educated but not very adept at fitting in socially. He was an engineer often hired to design a part for an automobile or aircraft, and then not hired back. We had cycles with great amounts of money for a few months, then no money for a few more. We moved frequently to new locations for his new jobs. My mother saved and we always squeaked by. As a child I never knew any of this. My sisters and brother and I played cards, and built puzzles, and I made paper dolls. These things were fun and didn't cost a lot of money.

Do you remember your college days, or the first time you lived in your own apartment? Did you ever have more than enough money to get by? I lived in a one-bedroom apartment with old wooden Seven-Up boxes for bookcases. Life was simpler then. I didn't have a lot of money but I was very happy. Why is that? Perhaps I realized how important independence was and I had not let the troubles of the world overpower me.

As an adult, before Religious Science, I would agonize about how I could barely pay my bills. It seemed as though there was never any money left over. I carried that same mindset until I was forty-four years old and found the Bonita Church of Religious Science, the Center for Joyful Living. Then, in Science of Mind classes, I learned a new and more positive way to look at my finances. I learned to praise the fact that I could pay my bills, and that when I needed money to buy a house there were people who trusted me enough to give me credit. I started affirming that I had more than enough money for my wants and needs. Say it out loud right now, "I have more than enough money for all my wants and needs." Continue saying this for the next few weeks.

I started believing that money comes in many ways, from many sources, not just from my job. I started believing, as the Karen Drucker song goes, "God is my Source, God is my Power, God gives me everything I need." Say that out loud, "God is my Source, God is my Power, God gives me everything I need." Say it over and over for the next few weeks. In his book, *The Seat of the Soul*, Gary Zukav instructs us to

> *Take your hands off the steering wheel. Be able to say to the Universe,*
>
> *"Thy will be done," and to know it within your intentions. Spend time in this thought. Consider what it means to say, "Thy will be done," and allow your life to go into the hands of the Universe completely. The final piece of reaching for authentic power is releasing your own to a higher form of wisdom.* (239)

That's what we mean by affirmative prayer. Speak your desire and then let go and let God. Trust the process.

What about a troubled relationship or lack of harmony in the home? You have two choices: Do something about it or let it go. Try to talk in a calm manner about the issues bothering you. If you find you can't talk calmly on your own, go to a family counselor or therapist. Make an effort to see the best in the other person. Remember to praise your significant other or family member whenever you can do so authentically. If there is absolutely nothing they do that pleases you, why are you still together?

Byron Katie in an excerpt from her book *Loving What Is* claims you can change your life by asking yourself four questions about a persistent thought in your mind:

1) Is it true?

2) Is it really true?

3) How do you react and what happens when you believe that thought?

4) Who would you be without the thought? (16)

These four questions also apply to work situations. The bottom line: if something is not exactly right at work, are you going to feed it positive or negative energy?

What about illnesses or a lack of mobility? When you let go of worry, much of the tension that leads to illness dissipates. Maybe you can't, at this present moment, walk more than a mile, or maybe you have a hard time getting from your car to the house, but can you start improving mobility by walking in your yard one or two times each week? Can you increase your walks to three or four in the following weeks? Could you park your car in the farthest space from the market when you go out for groceries? Could you start doing affirmative prayer treatments for radiant health and flexibility?

Very seldom does a small child ever think he or she can't do something. Put healthy, flexible thoughts into your mind, knowing that with God all things are possible. And most importantly, remember the wisdom of Ernest Holmes when he referenced Matthew 18:3:

> **We must become as little children. How we long for a return of that simple trust in life which children have; in their minds there are no doubts—they have not been told that they are sinners, destitute of Divine guidance and spiritual life. The life of the child is lived in natural goodness. . . . We must return the way we came. As little children, who know that life is good and to be trusted, we are to approach our problems as though they were not. Approaching them in this manner they will vanish.** (*Science of Mind*, 456)

WORKS CITED

"Anyway," (an adaptation of the Paradoxical Commandments by Kent. M. Keith). In *Turning Hurts into Halos* by Rev. Robert Schuller. Nashville: Thomas Nelson, 2000.

Barker, Raymond Charles. *The Power of Decision: A Step-By-Step Program to Overcome Indecision and Live Without Failure Forever.* Marina del Rey, CA: DeVorss & Company, 1999.

Beckett, Candice. "Message from the President," *Creative Thought.* March, 2005.

Beckwith, Dr. Michael Bernard. *The Life Lift-Off Cards.* Boulder, CO: Sounds True, 2009.

————· *40 Day Mind Fast Soul Feast: A Guide to Soul Awakening and Inner Fulfillment.* Los Angeles: Agape Media International, LLC, 2007.

Bradbury, Ray. *Dandelion Wine.* New York: Doubleday, 1957.

————· *Something Wicked This Way Comes.* New York: Simon & Schuster, 1962.

————· "There Will Come Soft Rains." In *The Martian Chronicles.* New York: Doubleday, 1950.

Butterworth, Eric. *Spiritual Economics: The Principles and Process of True Prosperity.* Unity Village, MO: Unity School of Christianity, 1983.

Byrnes, Rhonda. *The Power.* New York: Atria Books, 2010. Kindle edition.

Callory, Paul. "Something Inside Us Knows." In *All Is Well,* by David Bruner and Lee Hartley. Los Gatos, CA: Hartley Publishing, 2010.

Campbell, Dr. Patricia. *Giving God A Good Time.* Temecula, CA: Knotty Rev Publishers, 2010.

Canfield, Jack and Mark Victor Hansen. *Chicken Soup for the Soul.* Hartford, CT. Deerfield Beach, FL: Health Communications, Inc., 1993.

Canfield, Jack, Mark Victor Hansen, and Les Hewitt. *The Power of Focus: How to Hit Your Business, Personal and Financial Targets with Absolute Certainty.* Dearfield Beach, FL: Health Communications, Inc., 2000.

Chapman, Gary. *The Five Love Languages: The Secret to Love That Lasts.* Chicago: Northfield Publishing, 1984.

Chisholm, Patricia. "Canada: an Extraordinary Capacity to Forgive: Vietnam Victim Phan Thi Kim Phuc Has Found Peace in Canada." *Maclean's* (February 10, 1997).

Chopra, Deepak. *The Seven Spiritual Laws of Success.* San Rafael: Amber-Allen Publishing, 1993.

Cole-Whittaker, Terry. *Dare to Be Great.* New York: Penguin Book, 2001.

————· *What You Think of Me Is None of My Business.* New York: The Berkley Publishing House, 1979.

Crapolicchio, Tony. "Changing the World One Thought at a Time," *Creative Thought,* March, 2005.

Crystal, Billy. "My Father and Me," *Reader's Digest,* February 2005

Dee, Peter. *Voices of the High School,* "Roger and Mary." New York: Baker's Plays, 1982.

Drucker, Karen. *Let Go of the Shore: Stories and Songs That Set the Spirit Free.* Camarillo, CA: DeVorss & Co., 2010.

Drucker, Karen. "God Is My Source," *Songs of the Spirit I*. Tay Toones Music BMI, 1999.

Drucker, Karen and John Hoy. "N-O Is My New Yes," *All About Love*. Tay Toones Music BMI, 2004.

Drucker, Karen and Karyl Huntley. "Face of God," *Songs of the Spirit II*. Tay Toones Music BMI, 2001.

Dyer, Wayne. *Being in Balance: 9 Principles for Creating Habits to Match Your Desires*. Carlsbad, CA: Hay House, 2006.

————· *Excuses Be Gone: How to Change Lifelong, Self-Defeating Thinking Habits*. Carlsbad, CA: Hay House, 2009.

————· *Getting in the Gap: Making Conscious Contact with God Through Meditation*. Carlsbad, CA: Hay House, 2012.

————· *Inspiration Cards: Your Ultimate Calling*. Carlsbad, CA: Hay House, 2006.

————· *Manifest Your Destiny: The Nine Spiritual Principles for Getting Everything You Want*. New York: Harper Collins Publishing, 1997.

————· *10 Secrets for Success and Inner Peace*. Carlsbad, CA: Hay House.

————· *The Shift: Taking Your Life from Ambition to Meaning*. Carlsbad, CA: Hay House, 2010.

————· *Wisdom of the Ages*. New York: Harper Collins Books, 1998.

Fillmore, Charles. *Metaphysical Bible Dictionary*. Unity Village: Unity Books, 2003.

Foss, Sam Walter. "The House by the Side of the Road." Accessed online at Poet's corner, the otherpages.com.

Gladwell, Malcolm. *Blink: The Power of Thinking Without Thinking*. New York: Little, Brown and Company, 2005

Harbula, Patrick. *The Magic of the Soul*. Thousand Oaks: Peak Publications, 2003.

Hay, Louise. *Gratitude: A Way of Life*. Carlsbad, CA: Hay House, 1996.

————· *Power Thought Cards*. Carlsbad, CA: Hay House, 1999.

————· *You Can Heal Your Life*. Carlsbad, CA: Hay House, 1984.

Hay, Louise and Friends. *Times of Our Lives: Extraordinary True Stories of Synchronicity, Destiny, Meaning and Purpose.* Edited by Jill Kramer. Carlsbad: Hay House, 2007.

Healing Spiritually. Boston: Christian Science Publishing Company, 1996.

Hicks, Esther and Jerry. *The Law of Attraction Cards.* Carlsbad, CA: Hay House, 2008.

Holliwell, Raymond. *Working with the Law.* Phoenix: Church and School of Christian Philosophy, 1992.

Holmes, Ernest. *The Hidden Power of the Bible.* New York: The Penguin Group, 2006.

————· *Living the Science of Mind.* Camarillo, CA: DeVorss Publications, 1984.

————· *The Science of Mind* textbook. New York: G.P. Putnum's Sons, 1938.

————· *This Thing Called Life.* New York: G.P. Putnum's Sons, 1943.

Jones, Dennis Merritt. *The Art of Being.* Simi Valley: New Reality Press, 2004.

————· Email messages, 2008 (call to IRS)

Katie, Byron. *Loving What Is.* New York: Three Rivers Press, 2002.

Keil, Jeanette. *Invitation to Wellness.* Carlsbad, CA: Hay House, 1984.

Kelly-Gangi, Carol. *The Dalai Lama: His Essential Wisdom.* New York: Fall River Press, 2007.

Larson, Christian D. *The Optimist Creed and Other Inspirational Classics.* New York: Tarcher/Penguin, 2012.

Levinson, Sam. "Time Tested Beauty Tips." Accessed on englishteachernet.blogspot.com.

Markova, Dawn. *Random Acts of Kindness.* San Francisco: Canari Press, 2002. Kindle edition.

Millay, Edna St. Vincent. *The Buck in the Snow and Other Poems.* New York: Harper Row, 1928.

Morrissey, Mary. *Prosperity Plus DVD.* 2013 LSTW, LLC.

Moses, Jeffery. *Oneness; Great Principles Shared by All Religions.* New York: Ballantine Books, 1989.

Olfson, Lewy. *Great Caesar's Ghost* in Plays magazine, March 1973.

Proctor, Bob. *You Were Born Rich*. Scottsdale: LifeSuccess Productions, 1997.

Reynolds, Caroline. *Spiritual Fitness: How to Live in Truth and Trust*. Camarillo, CA: DeVorss Publishing, 2005.

Remen, Rachel Naomi, MD. *Kitchen Table Wisdom: Stories That Heal*. New York: Riverhead Books, 2006.

Ruiz, Don Miguel. The Four Agreements: *A Practical Guide to Personal Freedom*. San Rafael: Amber-Allen Publishing, 1997.

————· *The Fifth Agreement: A Practical Guide to Self-Mastery*. San Rafael: Amber-Allen Publishing, 2010.

Starke, William. *It's All God: The Flower and the Fertilizer*. Boerne, TX: Guadalupe Press, 1998.

Thurber, James. "The Unicorn in the Garden." In *Fables for Our Times*. New York: Harper Brothers, 1940.

Tolle, Eckhart. *A New Earth*. New York: Penguin Group, 2005.

Vosper, Frank. *Love from a Stranger*. Hollywood: Samuel French Inc, 1937.

Walker, David. *You Are Enough: Always Have Been . . . Always Will Be*. Camarillo, CA: DeVorss & Company, 2007.

Webb, Wyatt. "A Sense of Connection," in *The Times of Our Lives,* by Louise Hay, 216-19. Carlsbad, CA: Hay House, Inc. 2007.

Weldes, Petra and Christian Sorenson. *Joyous Freedom Journal: 365 Days of Inspiration*. Golden, CO: Spiritual Living Press, 2009.

Wilder, Thornton. *The Long Christmas Dinner*. New York: Harper, Collins, 1964. Play.

————· *The Matchmaker*. New York; Samuel French, 1954. Play.

————· *Our Town*. New York: Harper, Collins, 1938. Play.

Williams, Margery. *The Velveteen Rabbit*. New York: Doubleday & Co. 1922.

Williamson, Marianne. *A Return to Love: Reflections on the Principles of "A Course in Miracles."* New York: HarperCollins, 1993.

Zukav, Gary. *Seat of the Soul*. New York: Fireside, 1990.